Palm Harbor Library
2330 Nebraska Avenue
Palm Harbor, FL 34683

OFF-LOOM

Woven Bead Necklaces

Deb DiMarco

**Photography by Anne B. Lester,
Dana Gayner, and Deb DiMarco**

Schiffer Publishing Ltd

4880 Lower Valley Road, Atglen, Pennsylvania 19310

Other Schiffer Books on Related Subjects:
Flower Jewelry, Ani Afshar. ISBN:978-0-7643-2855-8. $12.95
Beads &Agate Jewelry To Make Yourself, Connie Wagner. ISBN: 978-0-7643-2998-2. $14.99
Knitting Beaded Purses: A Complete Guide to Creating Your Own. Nancy Seven VanDerPuy.
ISBN: 978-0-7643-2870-1. $16.95

Schiffer Books are available at special discounts for bulk purchases for sales promotions or premiums. Special editions, including personalized covers, corporate imprints, and excerpts can be created in large quantities for special needs. For more information contact the publisher:

Published by Schiffer Publishing Ltd.
4880 Lower Valley Road
Atglen, PA 19310
Phone: (610) 593-1777; Fax: (610) 593-2002
E-mail: Info@schifferbooks.com

For the largest selection of fine reference books on this and related subjects, please visit our web site at www.schifferbooks.com
We are always looking for people to write books on new and related subjects. If you have an idea for a book please contact us at the above address.

This book may be purchased from the publisher.
Include $5.00 for shipping.
Please try your bookstore first.
You may write for a free catalog.

In Europe, Schiffer books are distributed by
Bushwood Books
6 Marksbury Ave.
Kew Gardens
Surrey TW9 4JF England
Phone: 44 (0) 20 8392 8585; Fax: 44 (0) 20 8392 9876
E-mail: info@bushwoodbooks.co.uk
Website: www.bushwoodbooks.co.uk

Text © 2009 by Deb DiMarco
Photography © 2009 by Anne B. Lester, Dana Gayner, and Deb DiMarco

Library of Congress Control Number: 2009924395

All rights reserved. No part of this work may be reproduced or used in any form or by any means—graphic, electronic, or mechanical, including photocopying or information storage and retrieval systems—without written permission from the publisher.
The scanning, uploading and distribution of this book or any part thereof via the Internet or via any other means without the permission of the publisher is illegal and punishable by law. Please purchase only authorized editions and do not participate in or encourage the electronic piracy of copyrighted materials.
"Schiffer," "Schiffer Publishing Ltd. & Design," and the "Design of pen and ink well" are registered trademarks of Schiffer Publishing Ltd.

Designed by RoS
Type set in ZurichBT

ISBN: 978-0-7643-3306-4
Printed in China

Contents

Preface: Yes, You Can!

I hope this will be a "Can Do" not a "How To" book, keeping you, my reader, in mind. Off-loom bead weaving is not complex; but it does take patience. Each of the necklaces shown may be completed in a weekend, and the bracelets might take the better part of a day. The weaving itself will perhaps take 20 minutes to a half an hour per inch. It may seem like slow going at times, but remember, a bracelet is usually 7 to 8 inches, so even at the rate of 2 inches per hour, it would only take four hours to stitch an 8-inch bracelet.

The situation, as often as not, is who has four hours to sit down and "play?" The beauty of the projects I offer is that they are easy to work on in short bursts of time. If you have an hour to spare,

you can use it to weave a panel or two. Sooner or later you'll have completed enough panels to create a beautiful necklace or bracelet to wear or to give as a gift.

I invite you to use this book not only to learn the patterns shown, but as a springboard to your own creativity. Simply because I've used blue to show a pattern doesn't mean you must use blue. If you prefer green, use green or red or yellow or orange. I encourage you to experiment. Go off on tangents. Try new things. What I'd like to share with you, more than anything else, is the technique. While it might look complicated and produce eye-catching results, it is really a series of joining threads that, once applied, quickly becomes easy to do.

Let it be known that I never wove a bead, strung a bead, or made a bead before I was forty years old. That's right; I guess you could say I'm a late bloomer. As a matter of fact, I hardly thought of beads at all unless they were attached to ear wires and generally found at "hand made" crafts shops with an expensive price tag attached. The organic quality of artisan jewelry appealed to me, as well as possessing items that were one-of-a-kind. After purchasing several pairs of beautifully crafted earrings, my wallet and I had a little talk. My wallet said, "Deb, you can do this yourself." And I replied, "I think you are right."

Being fortunate enough to live in a township that actually had a bead store, that soon became my favorite place to spend time. The young proprietress was quite helpful and accommodating, never seeming to mind that I would line up bead after bead, side by side, looking for the perfect match. After eliminating the orphans and making my purchase, I would rush home to lay everything out on the kitchen table and wait for inspiration to hit. It never took long. The next day I would proudly wear my new earrings to work.

But beads have a way of multiplying, especially if you hang around them too long, and that is exactly what happened to me. My few new sets of designer earrings soon grew to 20, then 30, then 50; and before I knew what happened, I had made

100 pair of earrings. What could I possibly do with them? Certainly, I could not wear them all! Thus, a business began.

The earrings were transported to the graphic design department of a large clothing manufacturer where I was employed. My earring sales that day were encouraging enough to ask if I could leave the jewelry rack on permanent display. Fortunately, the answer was yes. The little jewelry rack commanded quite a deal of attention; my fellow designers purchased gifts on a regular basis or when looking for something special to wear. I didn't exactly quit my day job, it would be years before I was ready for that; but I had been bitten by the bead bug and it wasn't about to let go.

For those of you who have also been bitten, you know what I'm talking about. For newcomers, very possibly you might find the same phenomenon happening to you. No need to call Beaders Anonymous, as confirmed Beadaholics have nothing to fear. Perhaps a few uncooked dinners are to be expected because the kitchen was otherwise occupied, or maybe the dinning room table cannot be found beneath the copious quantity of "stuff" you've acquired. If you happen to find yourself just a bit overwhelmed, remember these words of advice, which may help you as they helped me: "Relax, it's all good."

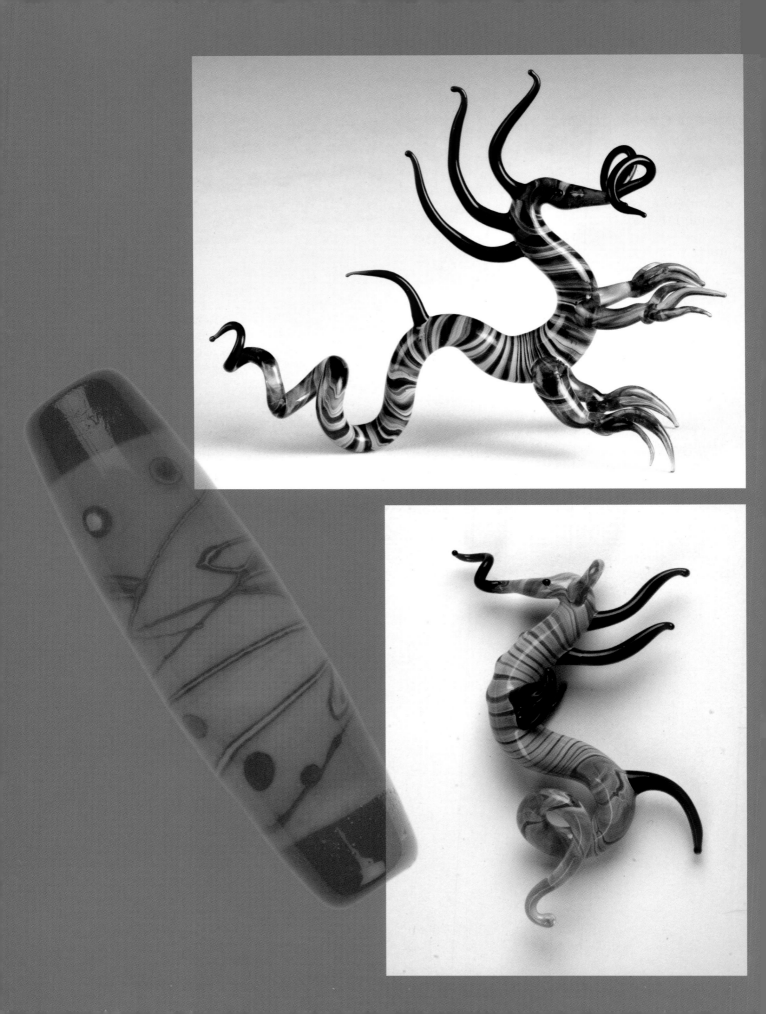

Acknowledgments

In October of 1999, I finally decided to quit my day job. It was the turn of the century and I had spent the past twenty years in the field of offset printing. Newspaper inserts, statement stuffers, posters, and brochures were the products of my trade. As a color specialist, a good deal of my time was spent in the manufacturing plants of huge print facilities; web presses roaring, sounding like giant, indoor, stationary trains. It could be an exciting business and often was. However, the past ten years had been spent on-the-road, and all of a sudden it seemed that almost half of my (hopefully) allotted years on earth were over. I wanted a break. I needed to slow down, take a good look at myself, and figure out what to do with the rest of my life. I guess I was going through a genuine, unofficial, mid-life crisis. To welcome in the New Year, I left printing to pursue more personal, artistic interests. For this I'd like to thank Gino and Nick who opened the door to opportunity for me, more than once. Thanks guys!

It was about that time that Victoria Gray Harding showed up in my life, and I thank her for believing in me and fostering a "can do" attitude. She is singularly responsible for my introduction to the South Jersey Bead Society, where I learned more about beads, beading, and beaders in a few short months than I had in several previous years. Victoria suggested that I spend some of my newly found time painting the kitchen and dining room of her Victorian home, generously offering to supplement my unemployment check. I accepted her offer. We spent a good month together becoming friends; me climbing over furniture, on countertops, and up ladders to reach the 10-foot high ceilings. Victoria was following a passion for beads by turning the parlor of her home into a business, The Bead Cellar, which, of course, was not in a cellar at all. Today The Bead Cellar is a busy and charming shop in Pennsauken, New Jersey, into which Victoria puts her heart and soul. Not only has she contributed generously to the creation of the projects in this book by her donation of supplies (including Toho™ seed beads, needles, findings and threads), but she has also shown unflappable confidence in me, more than I have in myself. She has let me want for nothing. Thank you Victoria, you help me believe in me.

A special thanks also goes to Anne B. Lester and Cathleen (Beach) Crewes, who brought over Thanksgiving dinner while I stayed home during the holiday weekend compiling this text. The support and encouragement of these two very special women is well appreciated.

Victoria's Bead Shop

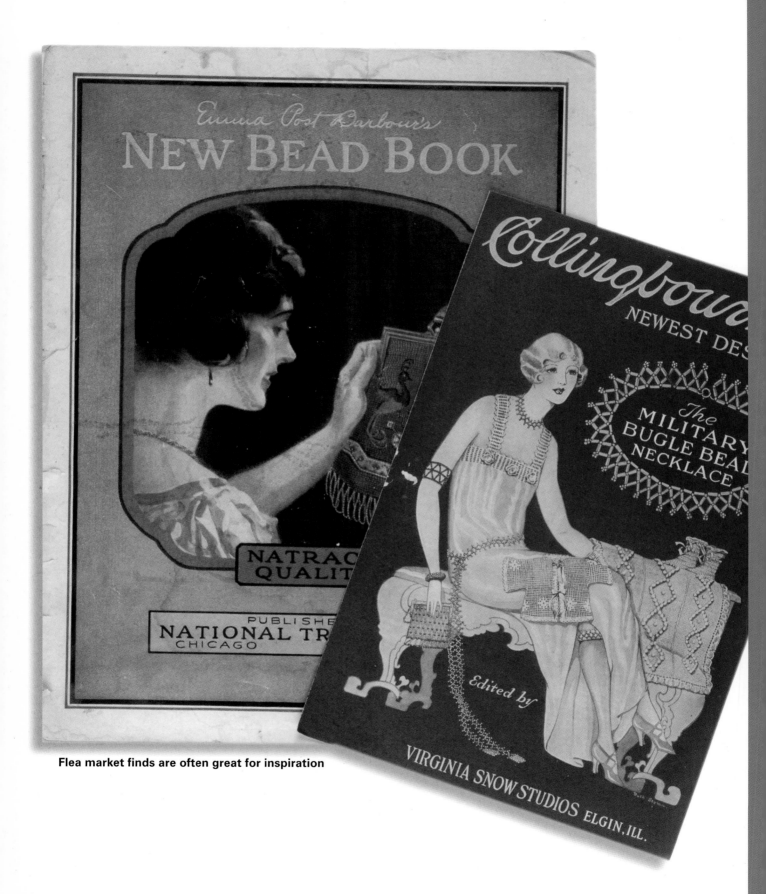

Flea market finds are often great for inspiration

Inspiration

The inspiration for this book comes from many sources. During the late fall and early winter months of 2000, I found myself the owner not only of a children's consignment shop but also of a rambunctious 40-pound (and growing) puppy. Mary Ann had stopped by the shop, introducing herself and her business: Skampers, a dog-walking service. My newly adopted pup, Jango, came to work with me every day and we were in the habit of taking a lunchtime walk. This meant closing and locking the shop during the half-hour break that rarely resulted in any lost customers. I couldn't justify the cost of a professional dog walker.

One day, Mary Ann commented on the jewelry I had on display and expressed how she liked my designs. She offered to exchange dog walks with me, explaining that she would like to give hand-made gifts to a group of five women friends. She asked if I would make necklaces for her to give as holiday gifts. We spent quite a bit of time together, discussing the personality of each woman and picking out color schemes. Not having any idea when I began where I would end, I surprised even myself. Thanks, Mary Ann, for helping set my imagination to seeking new ideas.

I'd also like to credit inspiration to John Stonis for saying I was his hero when I quit my day job. Thanks so much, Stonis, I'd never been a hero to anyone before.

And to my own two heroes, Jango and Abby, who both came to me by the way of the American Bouvier Rescue League.

Abby in clover

Jango decked out

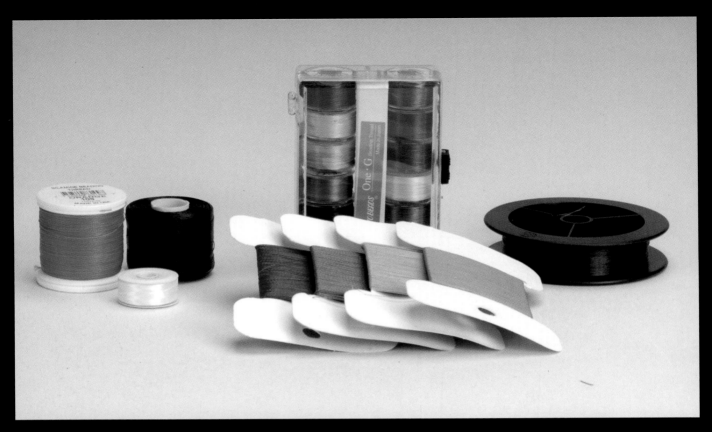

A selection of threads

Introduction

Off-loom bead weaving is easy to do. There is no fancy equipment required, just a few tubes of seed beads, accent beads, a pair of sharp scissors, needles, and thread. With a bit of imagination, patience, and a beautifully crafted clasp, soon you'll be creating sensational, one-of-a-kind necklaces and more. Off-loom weaving encompasses many different stitches and techniques, from brick stitch to spiral peyote.

My favorite stitch is the basic square stitch, which is used for the designs in this book. I enjoy the square stitch not only for its simplicity but also for its versatility and strength; plus, it gives uniform rows and straight edges, making it easy to create patterns and to add embellishments.

All the patterns in this book are clearly illustrated with four-color photography and text instructions. Although each woven design appears to be seamless, there are numerous joinings of many different threads. It is the joining technique that gives you the ability to master a seamless stitch. I encourage you to use these designs as a "jumping off" point for your own inspiration. Please substitute, elaborate, and change colors at will. As with any creative process, you should feel free to follow your own special path. I hope

that by showing you design techniques as well as patterns, you will develop the confidence to explore variations on your own.

When designing and selling one-of-a-kind products, we make a promise, not only to the customer but also to ourselves, that the designs will not be repeated. Please believe me when I say the creative well does not run dry. There will always be inspiration waiting around the corner. It might be in the form of a colorful hand-made bead or it could be a cloudy sky, a child at play, or an ocean breeze. Don't limit yourself; possibilities are endless when combined with your own experiences and impressions.

I'd like to share some suggestions that I hope will answer questions and help you avoid errors before they begin. This learning guide contains detailed instructions that show you how to master the stitches before moving onto the patterns. The text is arranged systematically, as one would encounter the steps when working through a project. Therefore, topics such as "Threading the Needle" appear before "Adding a Clasp." If you have trouble finding what you are looking for, please refer to the Index.

A beautiful clasp will enhance your design

Learning The Square Stitch

Selecting a Work Area

A work area is as individual as each person; however, it is a good idea to have a sturdy table and a comfortable chair. Although part of the charm of off-loom weaving is that you CAN take it anywhere, should you decide to sit cross-legged on a beach blanket, with the wear and tear on your spine, you might find yourself saying "Hello, backache!" after a while. I occasionally tend to move my work area with the weather: outside in the spring and summer or in front of the living room fireplace when the weather turns cold. Even though I have a spare room that, theoretically, could serve as a studio, my favorite workspace is still on the dining room table.

Gathering Supplies

A Good Lamp. Good light is always a good idea. It will help you see and save wear and tear on your eyes.

Sharp Scissors. I can't emphasize enough the need for a pair of good, sharp scissors. Small scissors are fine, and can be founds at a bead shop, a fabric shop, or craft store. A word of warning, do not use these scissors to cut anything except thread. Cutting anything else will dull the scissors and dull blades will fray the thread. Frayed thread is apt to show in your finished project and should be avoided to keep your work looking neat and clean.

Jewelry Pliers. Jewelry pliers are also available at bead shops, as well as fabric and craft stores. A pair of round nose, flat nose, bent tip and needle nose pliers are good for a start. If you'll be working with wire, then add a pair of wire nippers as well. Most bead shops and crafts stores carry economical sets.

A Ruler or any other tool for measuring.

A Non-abrasive Work Surface- Everyone seems to find what works for them, but personally, I like using a clean white dish towel as a work surface where I spread out my supplies. The waffle weave type work best for me; the little pockets hold beads nicely and the towel protects not only my table surface, but the beads as well. The weave of the towel can also serve as a measure if it has a graphic design such as stripes or checks.

Bead Trays (optional). Some people prefer to keep the bead colors separate. I start out with individual piles of color placed directly on the towel and eventually they tend to mix. If you chose to keep your colors separate, little bead trays are available from most supply shops. I personally like picking my beads up directly from the towel and am not bothered by them mixing.

Magnifying Lenses, if needed. The Toho™ beads I work with are so tiny that you may find a magnifying lens will be helpful. Dollar stores are a good place to pick some up. Further magnification may be found with a jeweler's lens, known as an Optivisor™.

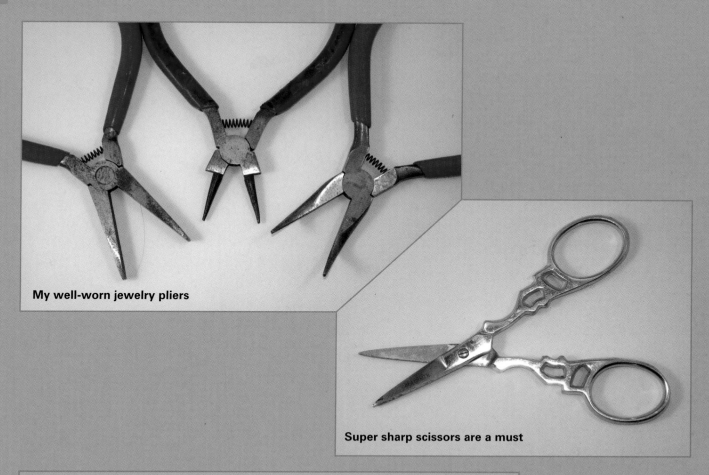

My well-worn jewelry pliers

Super sharp scissors are a must

The Optivisor™ jeweler's lens

Bead trays come in handy

Threading the Needle

Some of the beads for these designs are quite small, so the needles you use will be exceptionally fine. If you have trouble threading the needle, try this:

Look at your needle closely. There are two distinct sides to the needle's eye; the eye is round on one side and flat on the other. Threading from the round side of the eye toward the flat side will make it easier to pass the thread through the needle's eye.

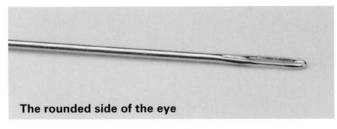

The rounded side of the eye

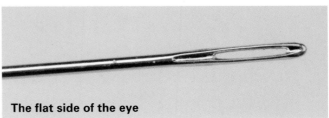

The flat side of the eye

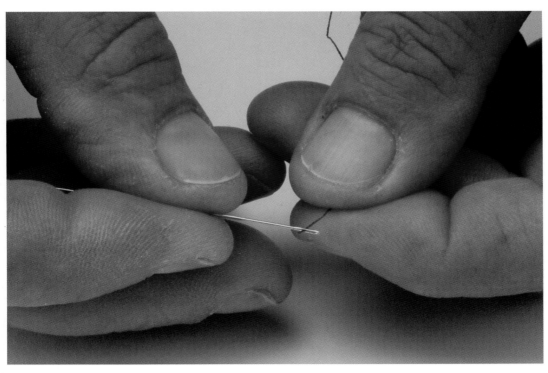

Bring your needle to the thread, not the thread to the needle.

Bring your needle to the thread, not the other way around, and be sure your thread has a clean, sharp edge. Attempting to put frayed, worn-out thread through the eye of a needle is a thankless task, while starting with a cleanly cut thread is a great time saver. The recommended amount of thread is the length of both your outstretched arms. Cut the thread flat, not on the diagonal; cutting on the diagonal will cause your thread to fray. I've been told that when having trouble threading the needle, moistening the eye of the needle can help. I tried this method and it seems to work.

When threading, hold the thread firmly between thumb and index finger, with just a spec of thread showing. Bring your needle directly over the thread and drop the eye of the needle over the thread. If you have trouble seeing the needle's eye, be sure you have good light and try working over a sheet of white paper. The thread is then doubled, with approximately one arms length becoming the tail. I do not apply beeswax because it adds unnecessary thickness and the thread I use is already pre-waxed.

Bent and Broken Needles

These superfine needles are quite flexible and may bend or break as you work. The bending torques the eye of the needle and makes threading difficult.

It is easy to straighten your needles, up to a certain point, by bending them in the opposite direction. Just grasp the needle firmly with flat nose pliers and gently bend in the opposite direction. This will realign the needle's eye, enabling the thread to pass through. Eventually, needles wear out. The eyes can get so compressed it is useless to even try threading them and if the point has dulled, they should be discarded as a matter of course. Be prepared to change needles often, as they not only bend, they break as well. Please always use and discard needles in a safe and secure manner. Curious children and pets (especially pets looking for food) are to be considered when you dispose of all your beading supplies.

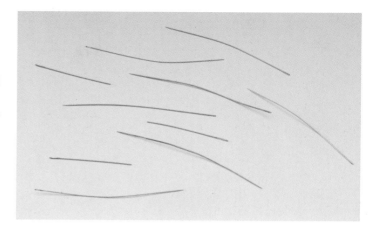

The superfine needles will bend and break as you work

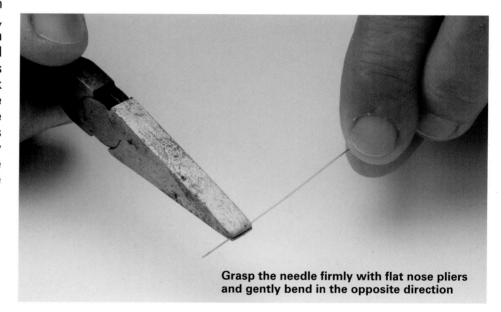

Grasp the needle firmly with flat nose pliers and gently bend in the opposite direction

Choosing Your Beads

Although bead manufacturers pride themselves on the quality and uniformity of these tiny seed beads, all beads are NOT created equal. You will find that some beads are misshapen or irregular. When in doubt, take it out; the patterns shown depend on the seed beads being uniform in size.

You will also find that the finish affects the size of a bead. For instance, a number 11 matte finish bead will differ slightly than a number 11 transparent bead. Don't let this deter you from mixing beads, just be aware of the differences.

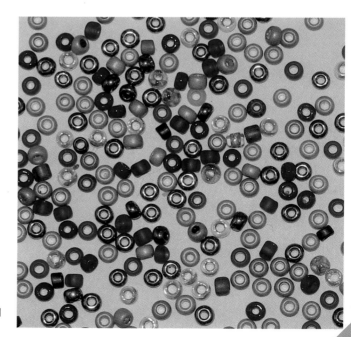

All beads are not created equal

Anchor Your Work

It will be easier to work the first few rows if you secure the thread of your work. Run a separate needle through a towel if you are working on one. Make a figure 8 around the needle with the tail of your thread. This puts tension on the thread and makes it easier to handle the first three or four rows. Turning your work after each row allows you to continue weaving in the same direction. After several rows have been completed, you may find it convenient to undo the tail thread from the figure 8 as you continue to work.

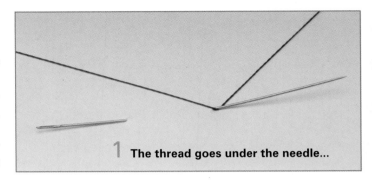

1 **The thread goes under the needle...**

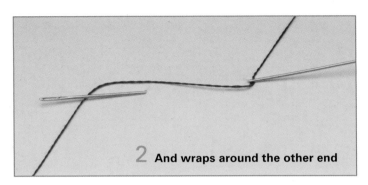

2 **And wraps around the other end**

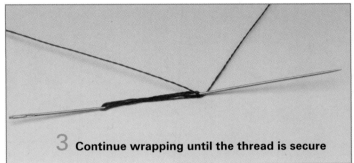

3 **Continue wrapping until the thread is secure**

Adding A Stop Bead

The first bead threaded will be used as a stop bead **and will not be counted as part of the pattern design**. To make a stop bead, pick up one bead on your thread, then pass the thread around and through the bead a second time. This stop bead will hold your first row of beads in place.

Stop beads will also be used as anchors during the course of weaving the pattern, so sometimes a stop bead will be called for when adding accent beads and may be removed later. Stop beads will occasionally remain in the design, helping to secure the work.

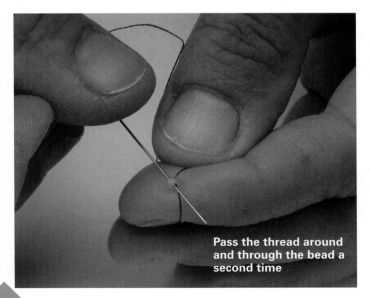

Pass the thread around and through the bead a second time

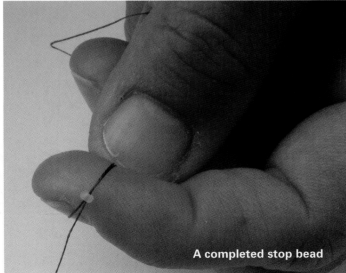

A completed stop bead

Weaving the Square Stitch:

Row 1

Begin with a stop bead. Then string on the required amount of beads for the first row.

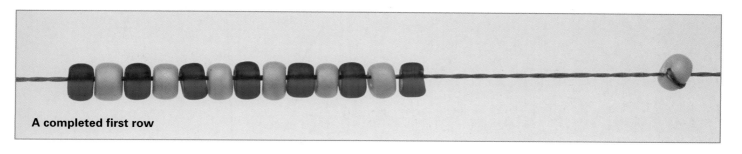

A completed first row

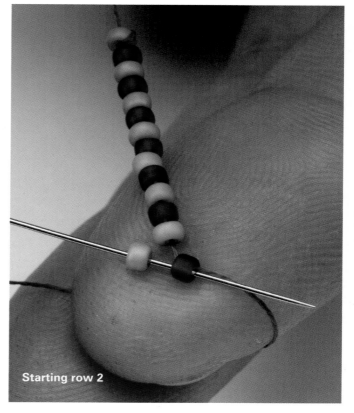

Starting row 2

Row 2

At the end of row 1, pick up one bead, then pass the thread through the last bead of the first row. Pull the thread tight and set the new bead in place.

Pull the thread tight

Pass the thread back through the first bead of the second row. Pick up one bead and pass the thread through the last two beads of the first row. Settle the beads in place. Now go back through the first two beads of the second row.

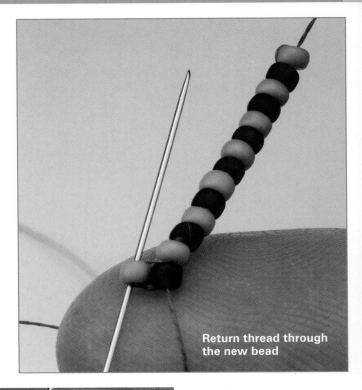

Return thread through the new bead

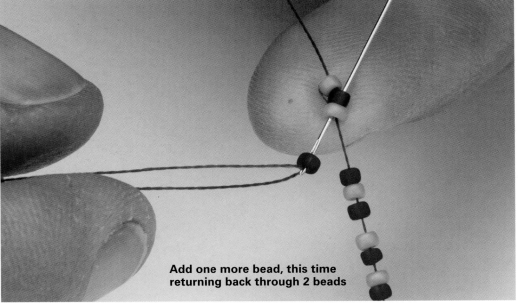

Add one more bead, this time returning back through 2 beads

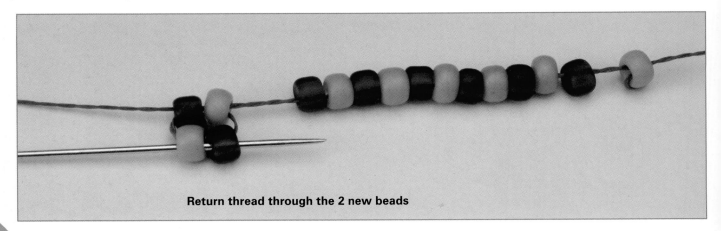

Return thread through the 2 new beads

Pick up one bead and pass the thread through two beads on the row above, then return through the two beads directly below.

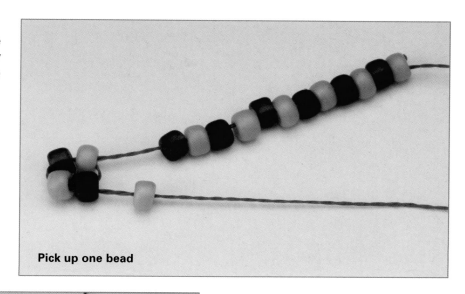

Pick up one bead

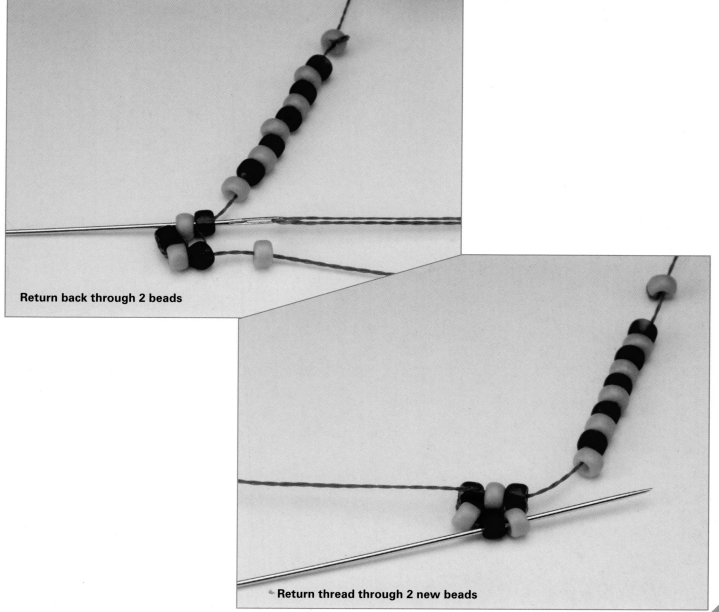

Return back through 2 beads

Return thread through 2 new beads

Continue weaving in the same
manner until the end of the row.

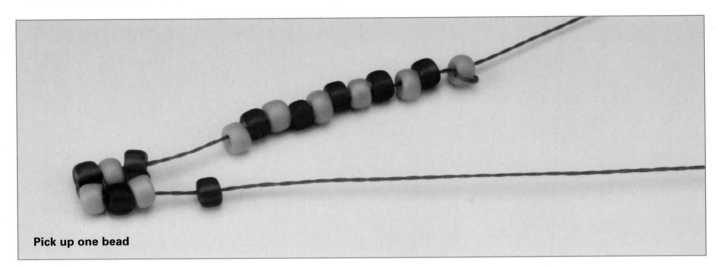

Pick up one bead

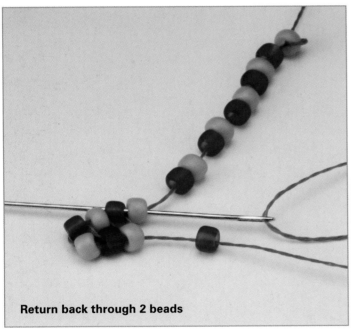

Return back through 2 beads

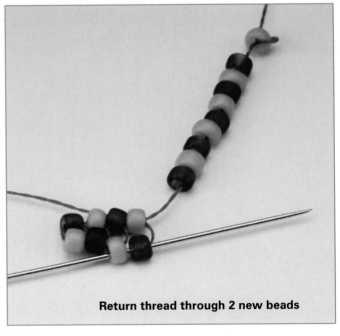

Return thread through 2 new beads

The completed second row

Row 3

When the second row is completed, pick up one bead and start again. To weave a straight panel, keep repeating this stitch until your pattern has reached the desired length.

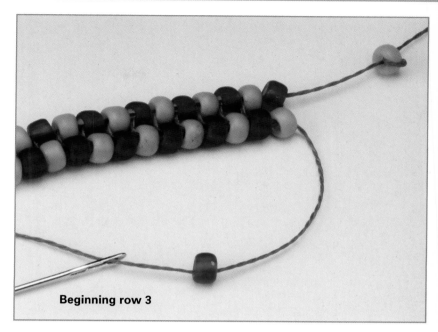

Beginning row 3

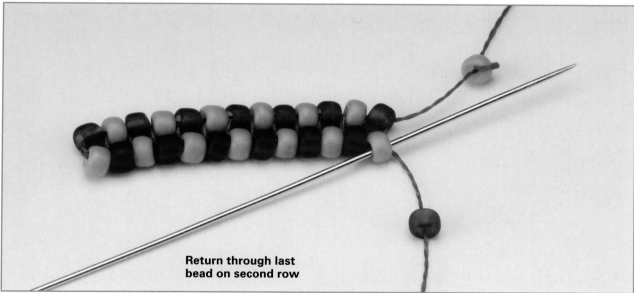

Return through last bead on second row

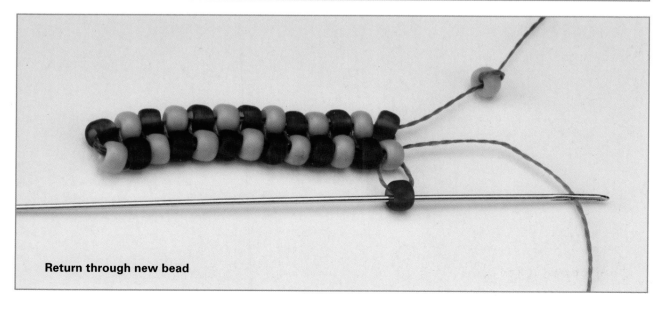

Return through new bead

Pick up one bead

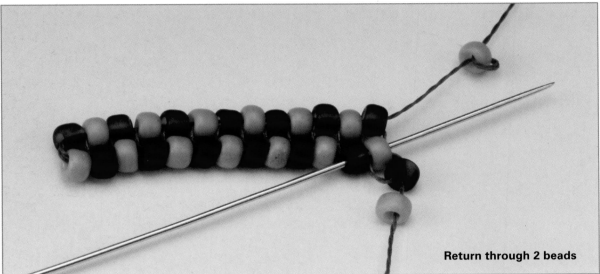

Return through 2 beads

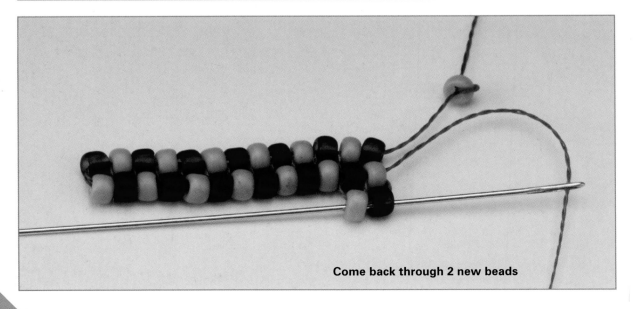

Come back through 2 new beads

Increasing and Decreasing Stitches
How to Lengthen a Row

A row may be widened or shortened by increasing or decreasing the number of beads. To widen a row evenly, increase by one bead at both the beginning and the end of the row. There are many possibilities when working with uneven widths. This technique provides opportunities to create a variety of designs. However, it is always a good idea to chart your patterns out before you begin. You may find they might need to be adjusted. For instance, in the example shown, I needed to make sure the light blue bead would come under the dark blue bead and not the other way around.

Pick up 2 beads

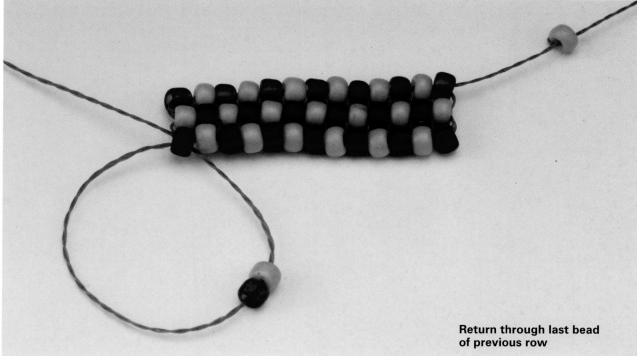

**Return through last bead
of previous row**

**Return through
2 new beads**

Pick up one bead

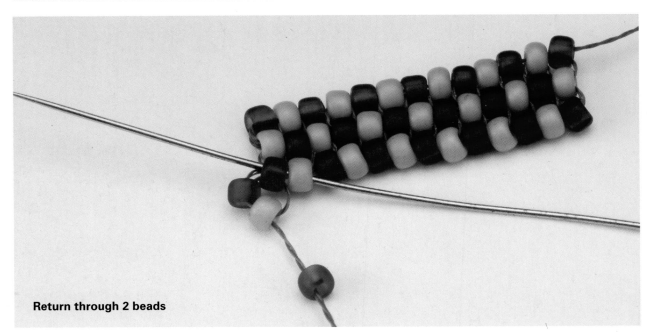

Return through 2 beads

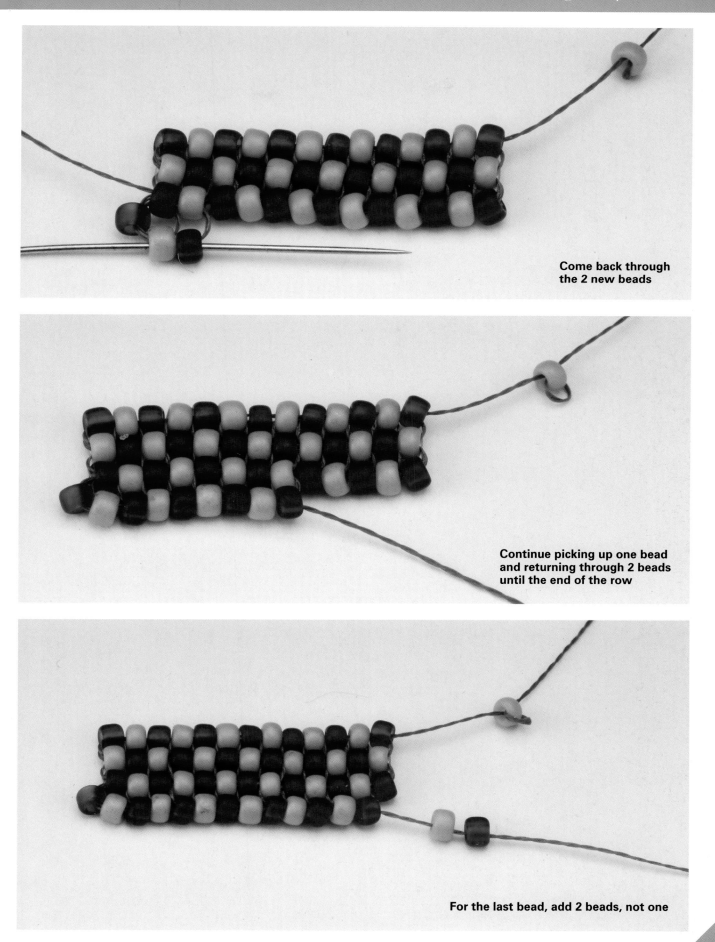

**Come back through
the 2 new beads**

**Continue picking up one bead
and returning through 2 beads
until the end of the row**

For the last bead, add 2 beads, not one

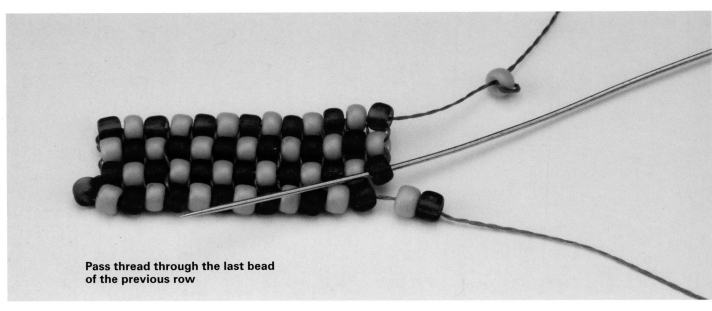

Pass thread through the last bead of the previous row

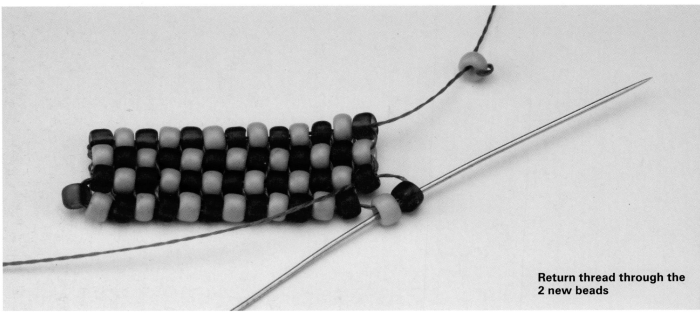

Return thread through the 2 new beads

The completed row

To continue at the beginning of a new row, pick up one bead. Pass the thread through the last bead of the completed row above. Return the thread through thefirst bead of the new row. Pick up one bead. Pass the thread through the last two beads of the previous row. Return thread through the two new beads. Continue the square stitch.

When starting another row of the same width, treat the work just as you would normally. Pick up one bead. Pass the thread through the last bead of the row above. Pass thread back through the new bead you've just added. Pick up one bead. Pass the thread through the last two beads of the row above. Pass thread back through the two new beads you've just added. Continue the square stitch until the end of the row.

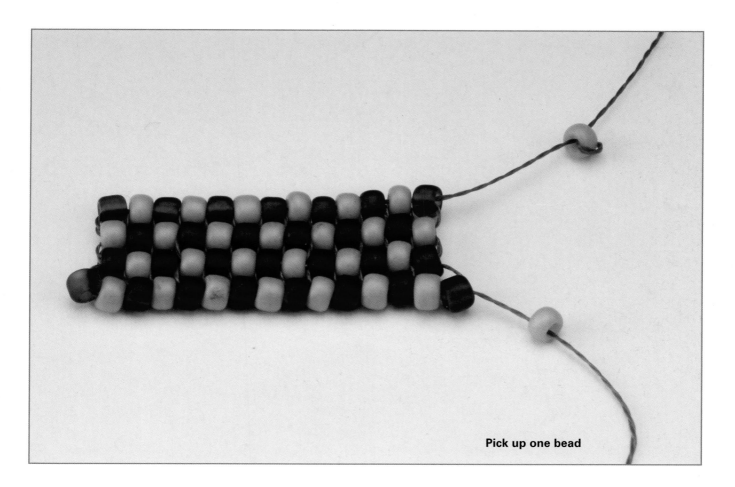

Pick up one bead

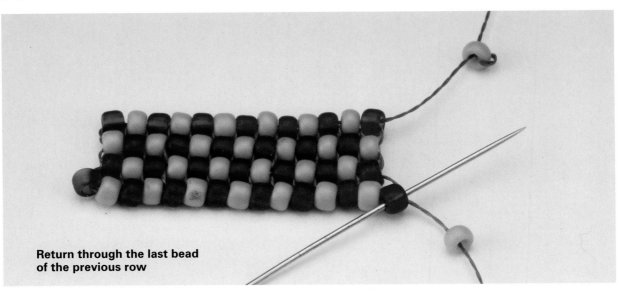

**Return through the last bead
of the previous row**

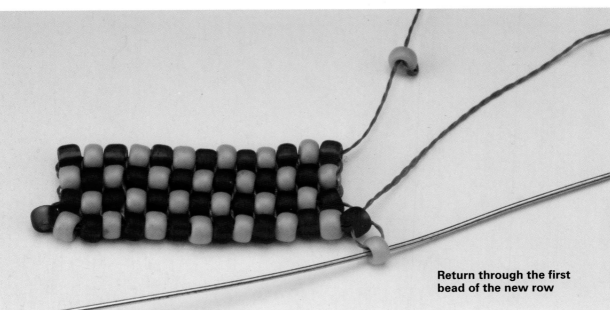

**Return through the first
bead of the new row**

Pick up one bead

Return through 2 beads on the previous row

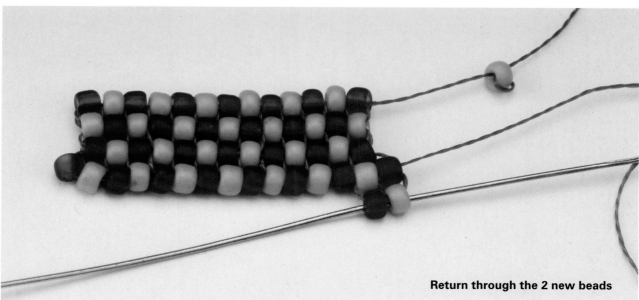

Return through the 2 new beads

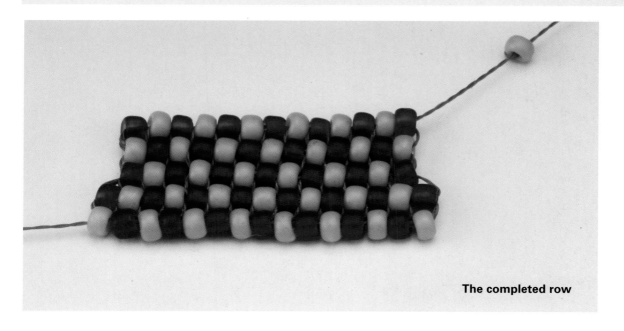

The completed row

29

How To Shorten A Row

A row may be shortened by decreasing the number of beads. To shorten a row evenly, decrease by one bead at both the beginning and the end of the row.

To decrease at the beginning of a new row, pick up one bead. Pass the thread through the last two beads of the completed row above. Pass the thread back through the first bead on the new row. Pick up one bead. Pass the thread through beads number 3 and 2 on the row above. Pass the thread back through the two beads on the new row.

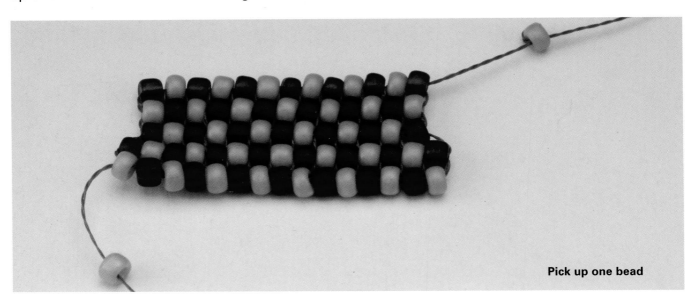

Pick up one bead

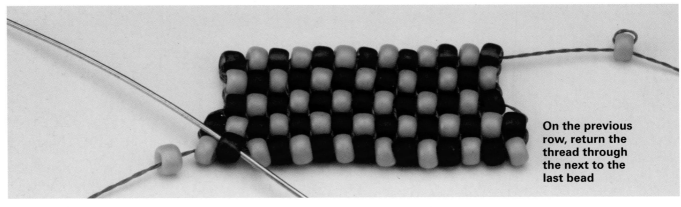

On the previous row, return the thread through the next to the last bead

Return thread through the new bead

Pick up one bead

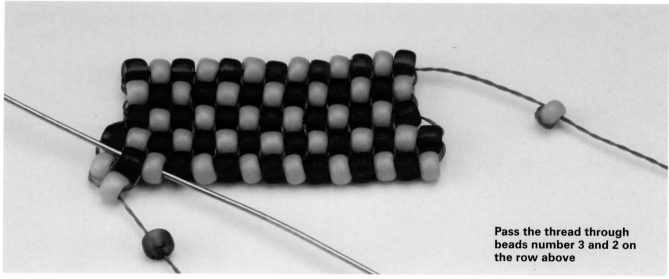

Pass the thread through beads number 3 and 2 on the row above

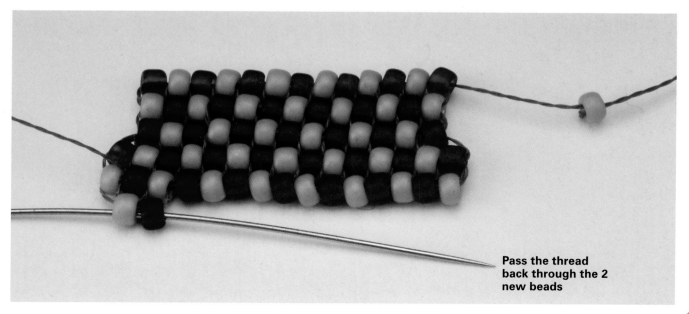

Pass the thread back through the 2 new beads

Continue weaving the square stitch until there are only two beads left on the row above. Pick up one bead. Pass the thread through the last two beads on the row above. Pass the thread back through the new bead. Turn the work and add a new row.

Pick up one bead

Return through 2 beads

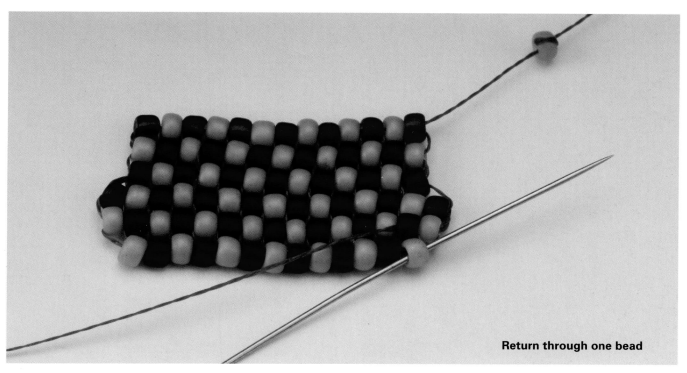

Return through one bead

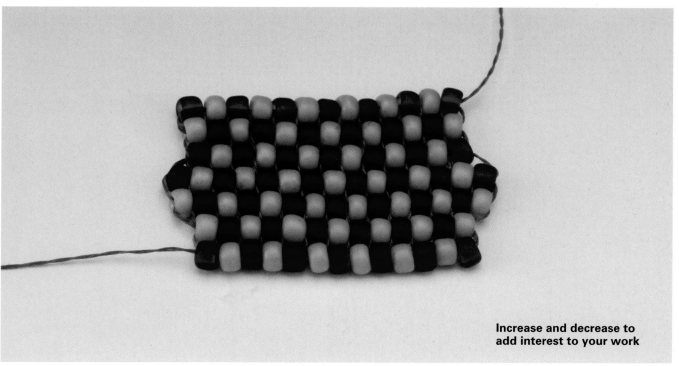

Increase and decrease to add interest to your work

Adding New Thread

You will be starting new threads many times as you work. I try to add new thread at the end of a row, unless increasing or decreasing beads on that row. In that case, add new thread in the middle of a row. It is easier if you plan ahead. Leaving too much thread is always better than not leaving enough. When you reach the end of a row, leave an 8-inch tail on your old thread. Begin your new thread a minimum of three rows above the last row. Much depends on the width of your weaving when deciding where to enter your new thread. On a wider weave, I recommend starting at least three rows above your last row; on a narrow weave, start five rows above. If you always use an uneven number your thread will exit properly.

Enter your needle through several beads toward the middle of your work, leaving an 8-inch tail. Moving down one row, pass the thread through several beads in the opposite direction. Reverse direction and weave through several more beads on the next row. Continue reversing direction and weaving down through your work until the thread passes out of the last bead on the last row. Give a little tug on the thread, it should be secure enough not to pull through.

Weave the 8-inch tail back into your work. Secure it by taking a back stitch along the way (see Backstitch). Always check your work carefully when adding new thread. When you start weaving again, corrections become difficult to make because once threads are woven in and trimmed, it is almost impossible to find them again. When you are sure no mistakes have been made, trim the old threads. Continue weaving the square stitch with the new thread just as if you were starting a new row.

The first time you run out of thread, you will only have one tail to contend with, but as the work grows the tails multiply, contributing to thread knots and tangles. It is a good habit to trim the tails as you go along. This is also an excellent time to check your work. If a mistake has been made, now is the time to catch it and correct it.

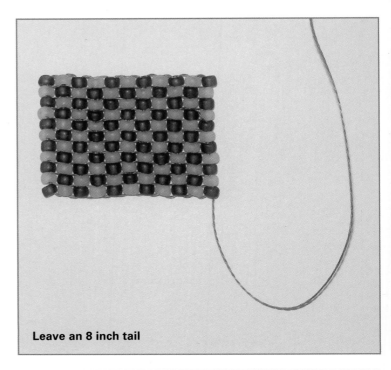

Leave an 8 inch tail

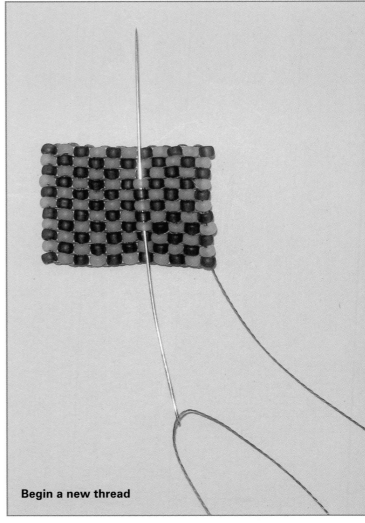

Begin a new thread

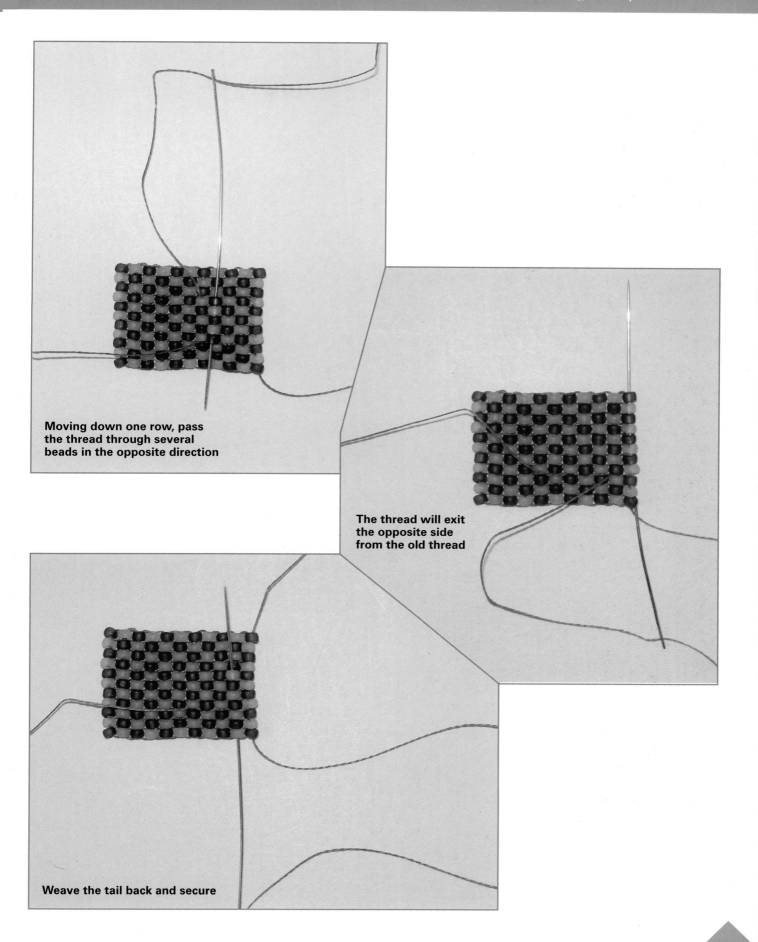

Moving down one row, pass the thread through several beads in the opposite direction

The thread will exit the opposite side from the old thread

Weave the tail back and secure

Back Stitching

Back stitching is used to secure the thread. You want to create a serpentine pattern by reversing direction and weaving the thread back through a few beads on the prior row. Then reverse direction again and continue weaving. This anchors the thread and prevents unraveling.

Avoid using the beads at the edge of the panels for weaving in loose threads and back stitching. This will keep those beads open for embellishment if you decide to add fringes or ruffles. It will also keep the visible threads fairly consistent in thickness. Remember, the bead holes will be used over and over when back weaving threads into the panels, so it is a good idea to set a pattern and stick to it. Too much thread in a hole could actually cause a bead to break when you try passing the needle through, so avoid overfilling the bead holes with too much thread.

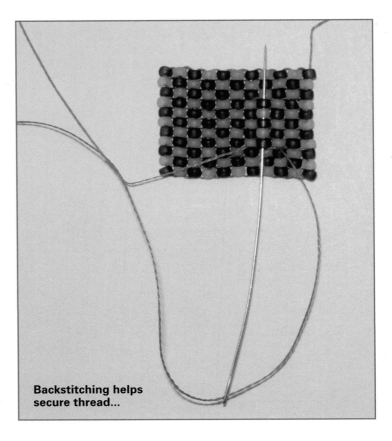

Backstitching helps secure thread...

Trimming the Thread

Super sharp scissor are the key to cleanly cut thread. Hold the work by the thread you wish to cut, putting tension on the thread. Position scissors squarely over the work, bring scissors close to the beads, and snip the thread. You should be cutting exactly where the thread exits the bead. Loose tension will result in threads that poke out and do not set into the work, and dull scissors will produce frayed edges. Take care with your cutting. Loose ends and frayed edges are difficult to fix and will mar the finished appearance of your work.

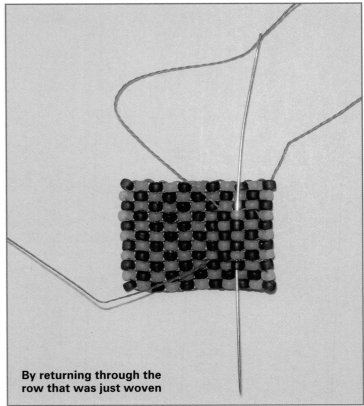

By returning through the row that was just woven

Common Mistakes and How to Correct Them:

Dealing With Tangled Thread

It is inevitable that at some point your thread might tangle. When it does, be gentle with the thread. If it has knotted, try not to pull on the knot. Examine the thread closely and try to locate the point where it has tangled and work it out. For knots, using the point of the needle to open them up often works. Avoid piercing the thread with the needle; this will weaken the thread and cause it to break. If all attempts to untangle the knot are unsuccessful, simply cut the thread, weave it back in and start a new thread.

A simple reason thread tangles is that it is too long. The recommended amount of thread is the length of both of your outstretched arms. The thread is then doubled, with approximately one arm's length becoming the tail. Loose tails in the work also create tangles. It is good practice to weave in and trim your thread tails as you progress.

An Extra Bead

If you've strung an extra bead, but have not yet completed the stitch, you can avoid unweaving your work by breaking one of the beads. I warn you though, do this carefully because it is possible to actually cut the thread in the process and end up unweaving more than you bargained for. To break an extra bead, use flat-nose pliers. Position the pliers at an angle on the extreme edge of the bead and squeeze, using short, sharp pressure. The bead should break and the thread should not be cut. To be on the safe side, bring the bead out to the end of the thread so if the thread breaks, all is not lost.

Broken, Frayed or Cut Thread

Don't despair. Unweave the work until you have enough thread to back-weave a tail, then start again using a new length of thread.

A Missed Stitch

Not only is a missed stitch annoying, but if it is discovered after your thread has been trimmed, it will be time-consuming to correct. So be sure to check your stitches at the end of each row and always before you start a new thread. If you find you have missed a stitch, however, it can be corrected. You must cut through the row of the missed stitch, sacrificing some of what you have already accomplished. This may be painful, but by doing so you will be able to unweave the thread until you have enough for a tail. Weave the tail back into the panel and start again using a new thread. This technique is useful if you are weaving a very long panel and have found a mistake. On shorter panels, however, it may be quicker to discard the panel with the error and simply start again.

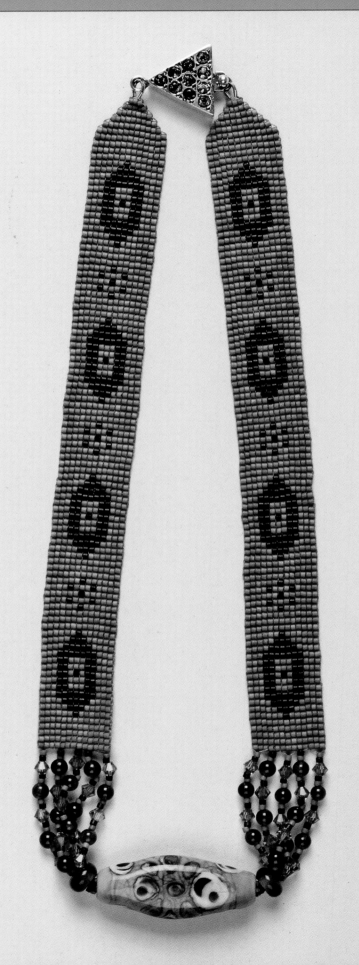

Purple Mountains Necklace

I love the tone-on-tone colors of this pattern. The isolated black seed beads really set off the light and dark purple pattern. The design is contemporary, yet based on a traditional one. The completed necklace reminds me of an Arizona sunset, with a Native American appeal in the duplex mountain design.

Estimated Time to complete: Approximately 10 hours.

The techniques used in this necklace will teach you about adding accent beads along with a focal bead, joining bead strands to the panels, and how to attach a clasp. **Please review "How to shorten a row" in the previous section before starting.**

Colors will be indicated as follows:
   DP for dark purple,
   LP for light purple
   BLACK for black.

Supplies for the Necklace

1 pack Toho™ Treasure bead #744 or similar cylinder bead (**DP**)

1 pack Toho™ Treasure bead #766 or similar cylinder bead (**LP**)

1 pack Toho™ Treasure bead #610 or similar cylinder bead (**BLACK**)

1 focal bead

2 spacer beads, sized to fit the ends of the focal bead

24 - 4 mm round amethyst accent beads or similar

26 - 4 mm light amethyst crystal bicones or similar

2 silver wire guards

1 sterling silver clasp

Beading needles size #12

40 yds. Silamide, dusty rose #195, waxed nylon beadstring, size A

Panels before adding the triangles

The Pattern

This design is based upon a measured pattern. It is a long panel and might take a bit of time to complete. Don't feel as if it needs to be finished all at once. Take your time; avoid "eye burnout". You will be adding many new threads, so it is a good idea to trim the threads as you go along to avoid knots and confusion. Remember to check your work carefully before cutting. If you find a missed stitch or a wrong color bead, it is often possible to undo the stitches and correct the mistake before adding new thread.

Start with two arms length of thread. Add a stop bead and anchor your thread. String on 13 beads and weave 2 panels, 13 beads across by 105 rows down. Each panel will measure 3/4 inch wide by 6-5/8 inches long. Small size adjustments can be made by adding more or less light purple beads to the ends of the panels.

Purple Mountains Panel

1st - 5th row: 13 LP
6th row: 6 LP, 1 DP, 6 LP
7th row: 5 LP, 3 DP, 5 LP
8th row: 4 LP, 5 DP, 4 LP
9th row: 3 LP, 7 DP, 3 LP
10th row: 3 LP, 2 DP, 3 LP, 2 DP, 3 LP
11th row: 3 LP, 2 DP, 3 LP, 2 DP, 3 LP
12th row: 3 LP, 2 DP, 1 LP, 1 BLACK, 1 LP, 2 DP, 3 LP
13th row: 3 LP, 2 DP, 3 LP, 2 DP, 3 LP
14th row: 3 LP, 2 DP, 3 LP, 2 DP, 3 LP
15th row: 3 LP, 7 DP, 3 LP
16th row: 4 LP, 5 DP, 4 LP
17th row: 5 LP, 3 DP, 5 LP
18th row: 6 LP, 1 DP, 6 LP
19th row: 13 LP
20th row: 13 LP
21th row: 13 LP
22th row: 6 LP, 1 DP, 6 LP
23th row: 4 LP, 1 DP, 3 LP, 1 DP, 4 LP
24th row: 6 LP, 1 BLACK, 6 LP
25th row: 4 LP, 1 DP, 3 LP, 1 DP, 4 LP
26th row: 6 LP, 1 DP, 6 LP
27th row: 13 LP
28th row: 13 LP
29th row: 13 LP
30th - 53rd row: Repeat from 6th row to 29th row
54th - 77th row: Repeat from 6th row to 29th row
78th - 100th row: Repeat from 6th row to 18th row
101th - 105th row: 13 LP

Decrease To Shape Triangle

After the last row, start to decrease evenly to form a triangle adding five rows of light purple beads to one end of each panel. Decrease by one bead at the start and one bead at the end of each row. The five rows will have 9, 7, 5, and then 3 beads. Using approximately 30" of thread should give you enough to leave a 12" tail for adding the clasp.

106th - 11 LP
107th - 9 LP
108th - 7 LP
109th - 5 LP
110th - 3 LP

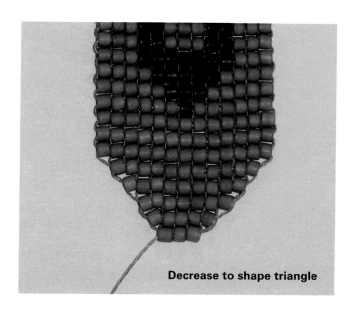

Decrease to shape triangle

Adding Thread for Accent and Focal Beads

Cut 5 lengths of thread, each approximately 30" long. These threads will be added to the flat side of each panel. Thread a needle and pass thread #1 through the 3 end beads, pulling through until the thread is an even length on both sides of the seed beads. Tie the thread into a square knot. Thread a needle and pass thread #2 through the next 2 beads, pulling through until the thread is an even length on both sides as before. Tie thread into a square knot. Do the same with the remaining 3 threads. Thread #3 will pass through the middle 3 beads, thread #4 through the next 2 beads and thread #5 through the last 3 beads. Tie each set of thread with a square knot.

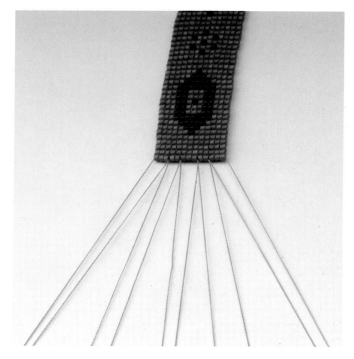

Add threads for accent beads

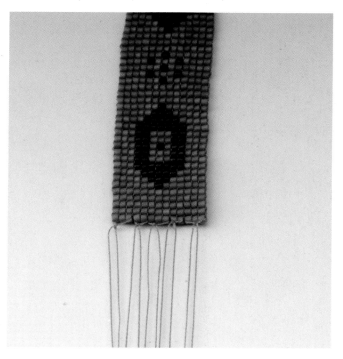

Tie each set of thread with a square knot

Adding Accent Beads

String the accent beads onto each set of thread. You may find it easiest to work one thread at a time.

For thread sets 1, 3 and 5: Use 3 crystal 4mm bicones and 2 amethyst 4mm rounds. String on beads in the following order:

> 1 LP bead, 1 DP bead, 1 crystal 4 mm bicine, 1 DP bead, 1 LP bead, 1 amethyst 4 mm round, 1 LP bead, 1 DP bead, 1 crystal 4 mm bicone.

Repeat until all beads are strung, ending with see beads. Make the last bead of each strand a stop bead. This way the accent beads will not slip off the threads as you continue to work.

For threads 2 and 4: Use 3 amethyst 4 mm rounds and 2 crystal 4 mm bicones. Sting on beads in the following manner:

> 1 DP bead, 1 LP bead, 1 amethyst 4 mm round, 1 LP bead, 1 DP bead, 1 crystal 4 mm bead, 1 DP bead, 1 LP bead, 1 amethyst 4 mm round.

Repeat until all beads are strung, ending with seed beads. Make the last bead of each strand a stop bead.

String on the accent beads

Accent beads completed

Release the threads from the stop beads and secure the threads with an overhand knot. A needle will help you move the overhand knot into place.

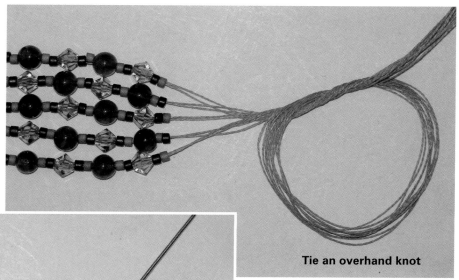

Tie an overhand knot

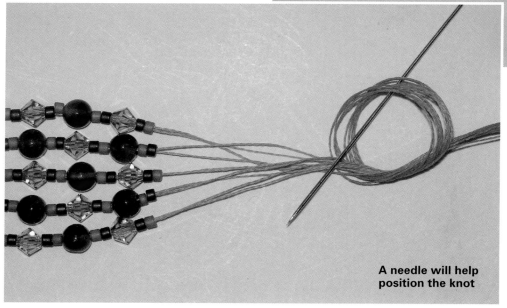

A needle will help position the knot

Add a spacer bead and seed beads

Add one spacer bead. Separate the threads back into pairs and add seed beads in the following order:

For threads 1, 3 and 5: Use 1 LP, 1 DP, 1 LP.

For threads 2 and 4: Use 1 DP, 1 LP, 1 DP.

Make the last bead a stop bead to keep work in place.

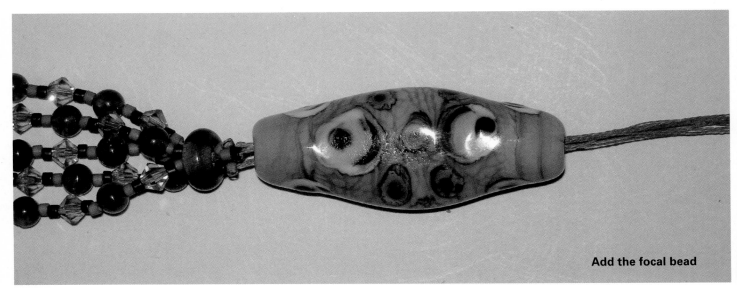

Add the focal bead

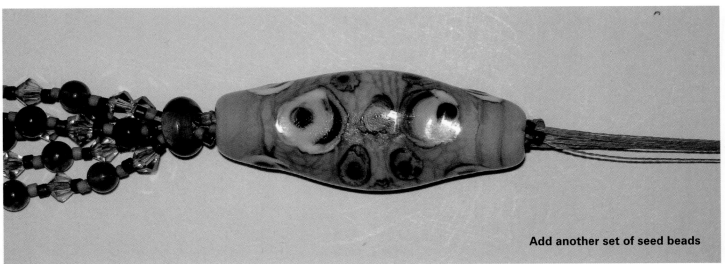

Add another set of seed beads

Separate the threads back into pairs and add seed beads in the following order. Make your first seed bead a stop bead:

For threads 1, 3 and 5: Use 1 LP, 1 DP, 1 LP.

For threads 2 and 4: Use 1 DP, 1 LP, 1 DP.

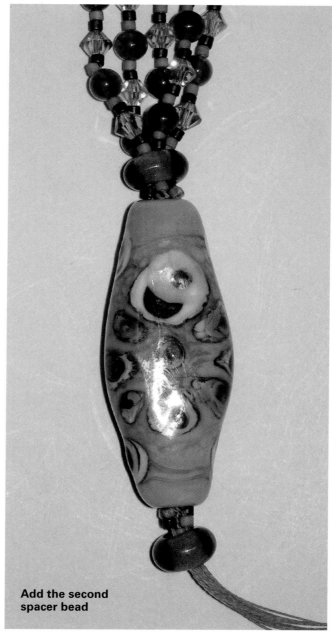

Separate the thread back into pairs. String the remaining accent beads onto the threads in the following order:

For thread sets 1, 3 and 5: Use 3 crystal 4mm bicones and 2 amethyst 4mm rounds. String on beads in the following order:

> 1 LP bead, 1 DP bead, 1 crystal 4 mm bicine, 1 DP bead, 1 LP bead, 1 amethyst 4 mm round, 1 LP bead, 1 DP bead, 1 crystal 4 mm bicone.

Repeat until all beads are strung, ending with seed beads. Make the last bead of each strand a stop bead. This way the accent beads will not slip off the threads as you continue to work.

For threads 2 and 4: Use 3 amethyst 4 mm rounds and 2 crystal 4 mm bicones. Sting on beads in the following manner:

> 1 DP bead, 1 LP bead, 1 amethyst 4 mm round, 1 LP bead, 1 DP bead, 1 crystal 4 mm bead, 1 DP bead, 1 LP bead, 1 amethyst 4 mm round.

Repeat until all beads are strung, ending with seed beads. Make the last bead of each strand a stop bead.

Add the second spacer bead

Add the second set of accent beads

Weaving Threads Back into the Panel

One by one, release the threads from the stop beads. Take each set of threads and weave the threads back into the remaining panel. Keep the same pattern as before. Your entry points should correspond with the opposite panel. Pass each thread of the set through the beads in the opposite direction. Thread set #1 will pass through the end 3 beads, set #2 through next 2 beads, set #3 through the middle 3 beads, set #4 through the next 2 beads and set #5 through the last 3 beads. Bring the thread sets together on the second row. Tie a square knot in each set of threads.

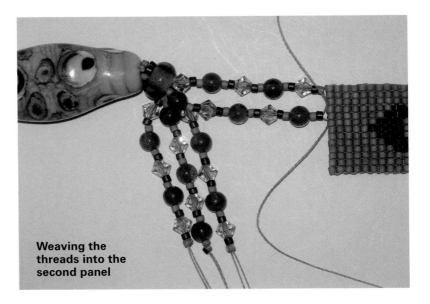

Weaving the threads into the second panel

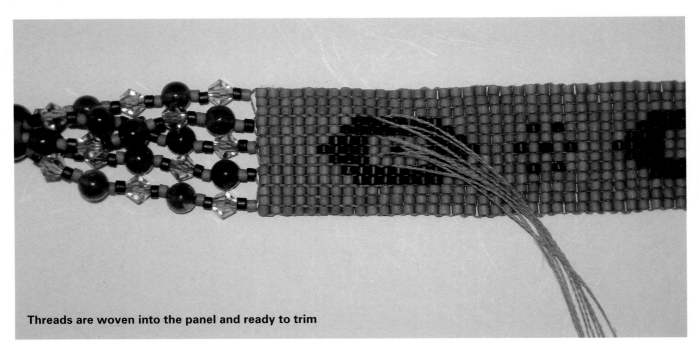

Threads are woven into the panel and ready to trim

Continue weaving each thread back into the panel. Be careful! Now is not the time to break a bead. If your thread meets resistance, find another path. As long as the threads have been tied with a square knot and back-stitched you need not weave further back than 5 or 6 rows.

Adding the Clasp

Using a wire guard when adding a clasp is the best way to protect the thread. String a thread guard onto the 12 inch tail of each panel's triangle end. Pass the needle and thread through the closed loop of your clasp. Return the thread through the last 3 beads. Pull the thread snug to tighten. Take several stitches through the thread guard and the last 3 beads before weaving the thread back into the panel.

A wire guard is used to attach the clasp

Reinforce with several stitches

Reinforce the triangle end by stitching back

Stitch from end to end

Row by row, weave the thread back through the triangle passing the thread through all the beads of the row. This extra thread will give strength to the triangle area and help keep the clasp secure.

When you have passed the triangle area, bring the thread out in the middle of the work. Continue to weave the thread back into the panel.

Take a backstitch or two along the way to secure the thread.

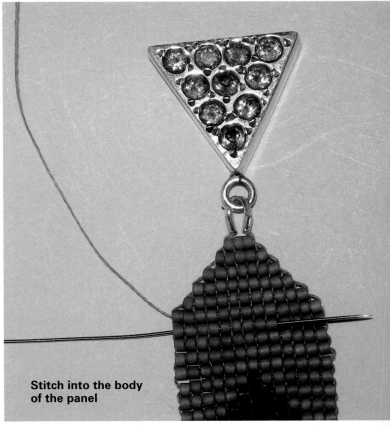

Stitch into the body of the panel

Weave threads into the panel

Trim thread once secure

When you have woven back about 12 rows into the work, cut the thread close.

Add the second half of the clasp in the same manner. Your necklace is now complete and ready to enjoy!

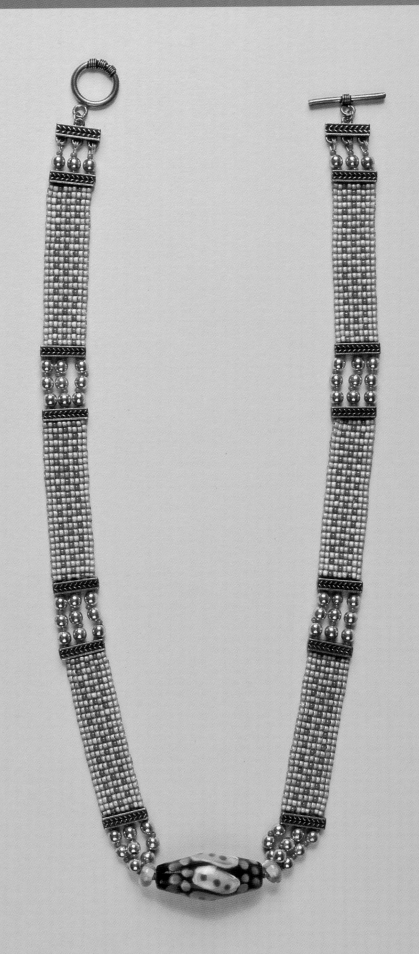

Autumn Harvest Necklace

This design is an example of simplicity at its finest! A repetitive, overall pattern creates a subtle mesh of color, accentuated by copper beads and findings. It is reminiscent of things both old and new. Drawing inspiration from the ancient Romans and Greeks, this necklace is a timeless classic.

Estimated Time to complete: Approximately 10 hours.

The techniques used in this necklace will teach weaving panels together using bar spacers and accent beads, adding focal beads, joining bead strands into a panel and how to attach a clasp.

Colors will be indicated as follows:

DO for dark orange
LO for light orange
G for gold.

Supplies for a 22-inch Necklace

1 pack Toho™ 11 round #46L bead or similar (**DO**)

1 pack Toho™ 11 round #562F bead or similar (**LO**)

1 pack Toho™ 11 round #557F bead or similar (**G**)

1 focal bead

2 spacer beads, sized to fit the ends of the focal bead

60 - 4 mm copper accent beads

12 - 3 hole copper spacer bars

2 - 3 hole copper end bars

2 copper wire guards

2 copper jump rings

1 copper toggle clasp

Beading needles #12

40 yds. Silamide, gold #7290 waxed nylon beadstring, size A

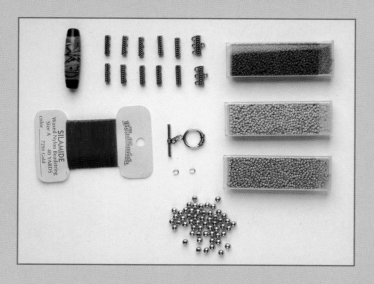

Use 4 panels for a 16 inch choker

The Pattern

This pattern has a variety of options. Using 6 panels will result in a 22 inch necklace and 4 panels a 16 inch choker. A bracelet may be made in the same manner either with or without a focal bead. The pattern is easy to remember; it is only two repeating rows and is highly adaptable to many colors.

Begin with a stop bead. String on 9 beads and weave six panels 9 beads across and 25 rows down. Each panel will measure 1/2 inch wide by 2-1/8 inches long. Size adjustments can be made by weaving the panels longer or shorter or by adding more or less accent beads.

Autumn Harvest Panel

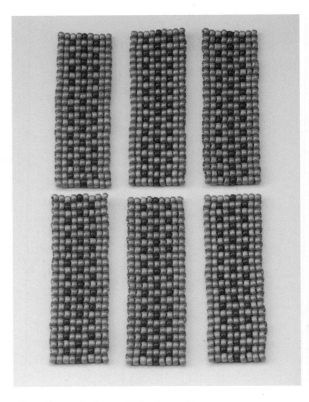

1st row: 2 LO, 1 G, 1 LO, 1DO, 1 LO, 1 G, 2 LO

2nd row: 1 LO, 1 G, 1 DO, 3 LO, 1 DO, 1 G, 1 LO

Continue the pattern until there are 25 completed rows or your desired length.

Use 6 panels for a 22 inch necklace

Adding Threads For Accent Beads

Cut 3 lengths of thread each approximately 20" long. Thread needle and pass thread #1 through 3 end beads, pulling through until the thread is an even length on both sides of the seed beads. Tie thread into a square knot. Do the same with the remaining 2 threads. Thread #2 will pass through the middle 3 beads, thread #3 through the last three beads. Tie each thread with a square knot.

Pass thread through 3 beads

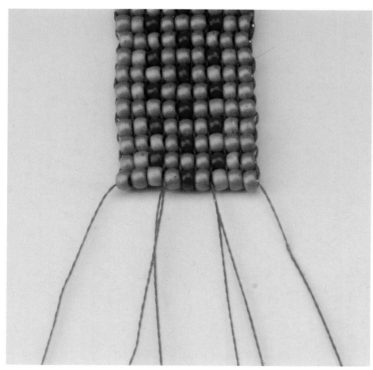

These threads will hold the accent beads

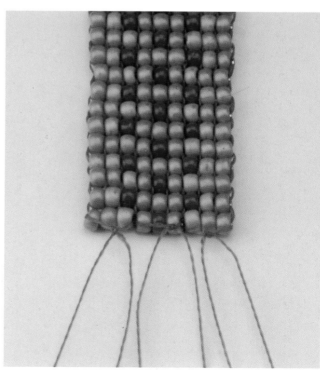

Threads tied in square knots

Adding Accent Beads

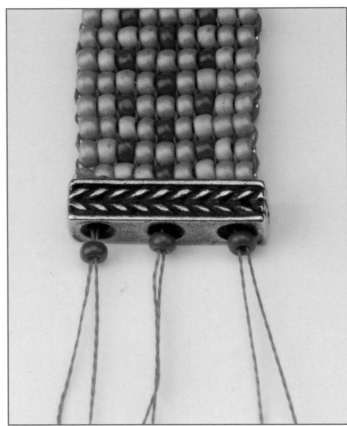

String 1 DO seed bead onto each set of threads

String a 3-hole spacer bar onto the 3 sets of threads

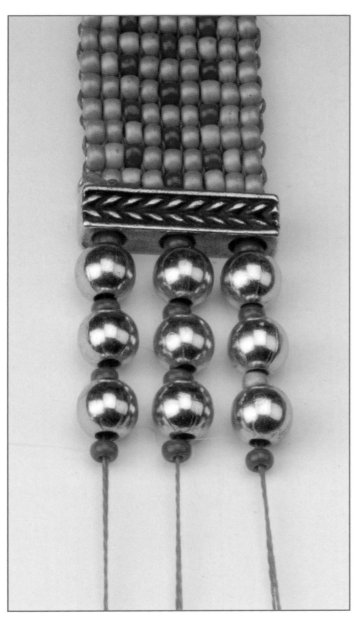

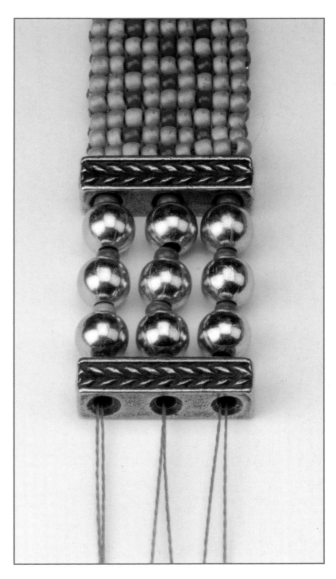

String a 3-hole spacer bar onto the 3 sets of threads

Alternating beads, string 3 copper accent beads and 3 DO seed beads onto threads, ending with the DO seed bead

Joining Panels

Join either two panels together for a choker or three panels for a necklace.

Take each set of threads and going in the opposite direction, pass the threads through the beads of the new panel. Each set will pass through 3 beads. Now return all threads to the first panel.

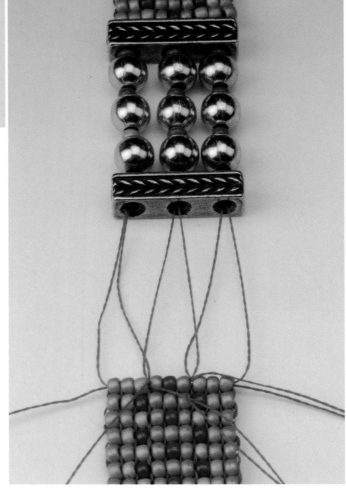

Begin joining the panel

Threads are now connected to the second panel

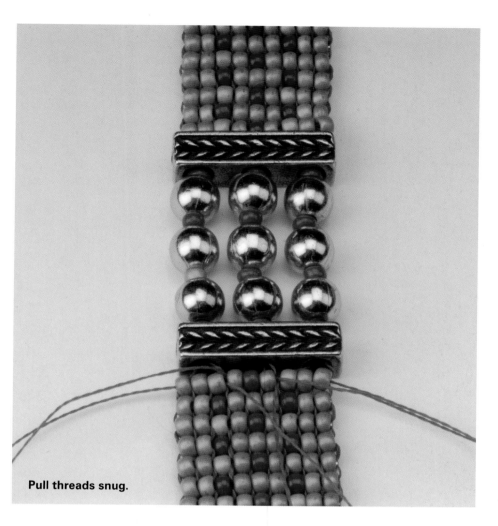

Pull threads snug.

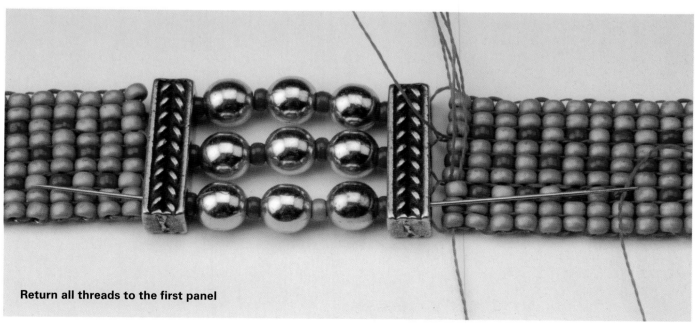

Return all threads to the first panel

The following photos will show how to weave the threads back into the first panel.

You will be ready to add the focal bead when you have two sets of panels completed.

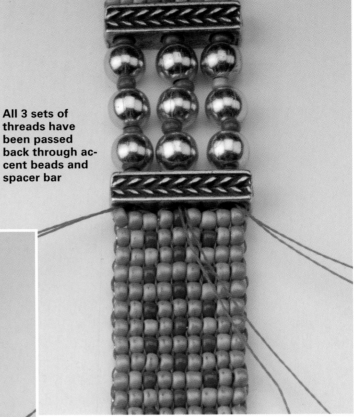

All 3 sets of threads have been passed back through accent beads and spacer bar

Pass the end thread through the 3 end beads, moving toward the middle of the work

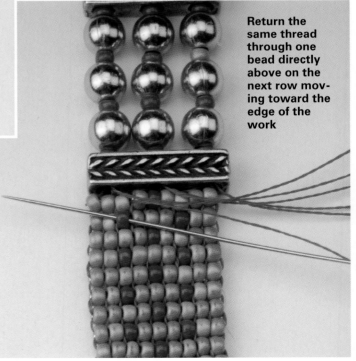

Return the same thread through one bead directly above on the next row moving toward the edge of the work

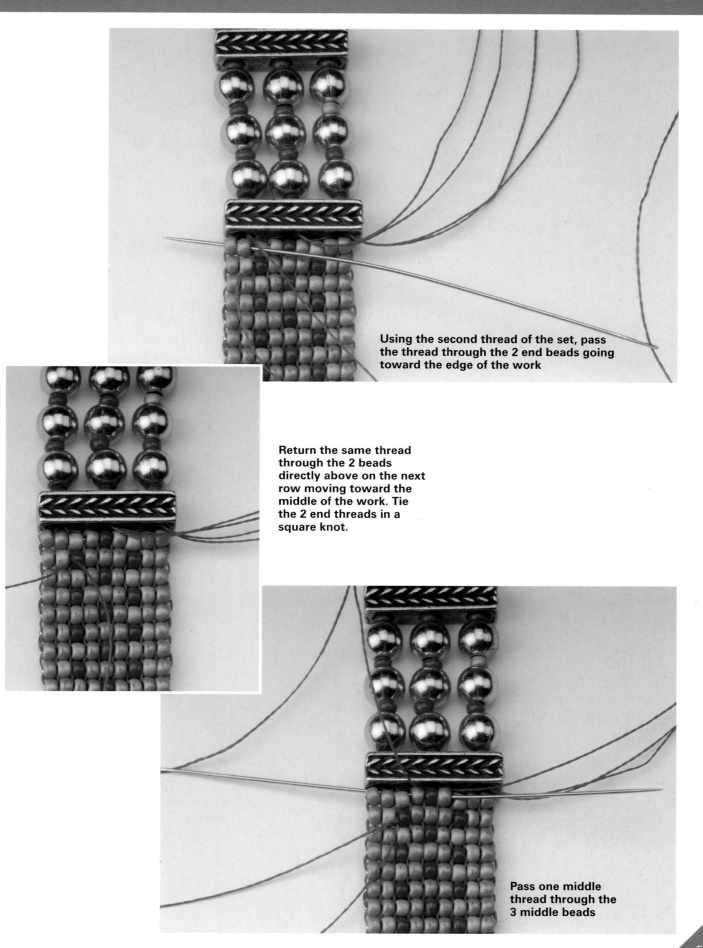

Using the second thread of the set, pass the thread through the 2 end beads going toward the edge of the work

Return the same thread through the 2 beads directly above on the next row moving toward the middle of the work. Tie the 2 end threads in a square knot.

Pass one middle thread through the 3 middle beads

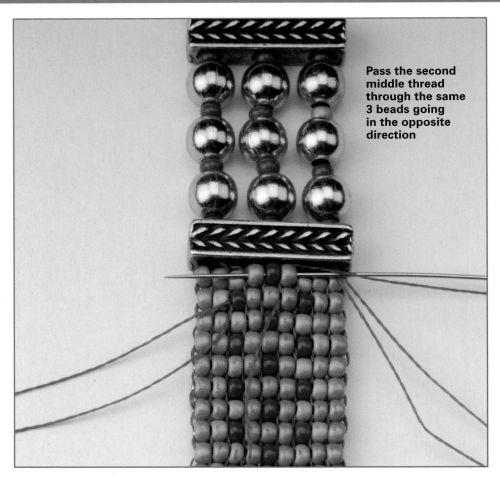

Pass the second middle thread through the same 3 beads going in the opposite direction

Bring threads together on the second row

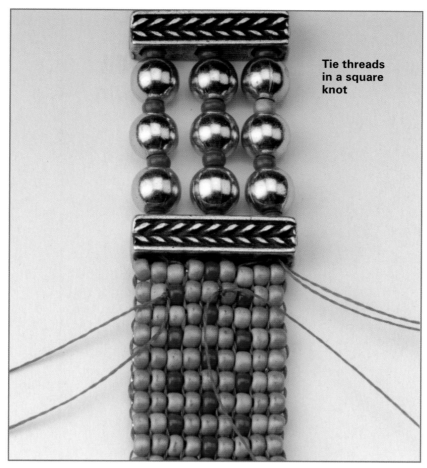

Tie threads in a square knot

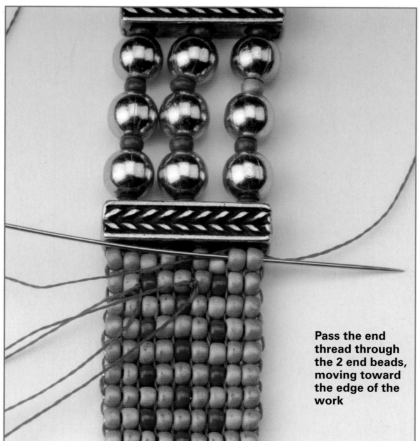

Pass the end thread through the 2 end beads, moving toward the edge of the work

Return the same thread through the 2 beads directly above on the next row, moving toward the middle of the work

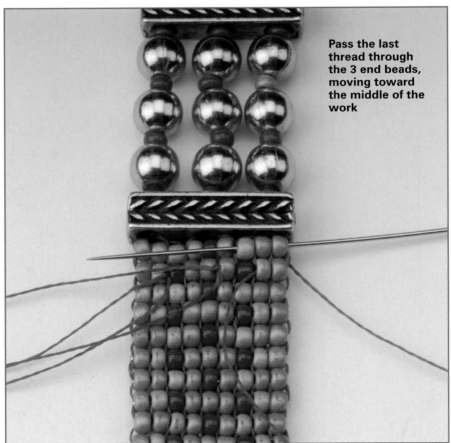

Pass the last thread through the 3 end beads, moving toward the middle of the work

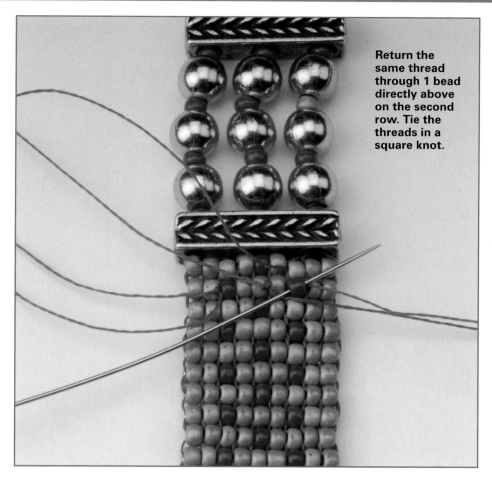

Return the same thread through 1 bead directly above on the second row. Tie the threads in a square knot.

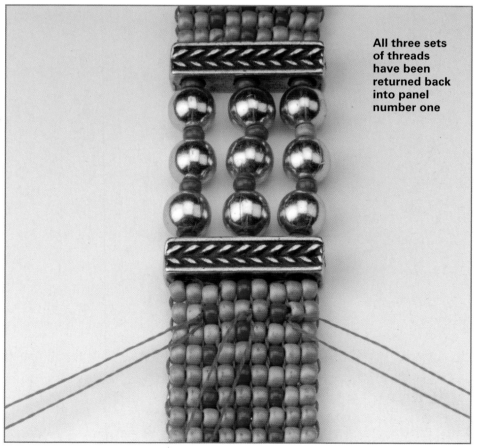

All three sets of threads have been returned back into panel number one

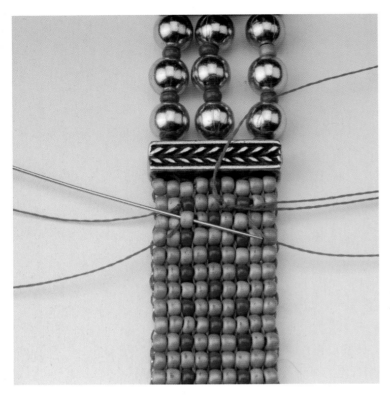

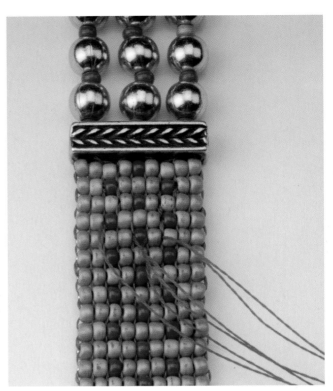

Continue to weave each of the 6 threads into the panel for about 6 rows, being sure to take a backstitch or two along the way to secure the threads.

All threads have been woven back into the panel

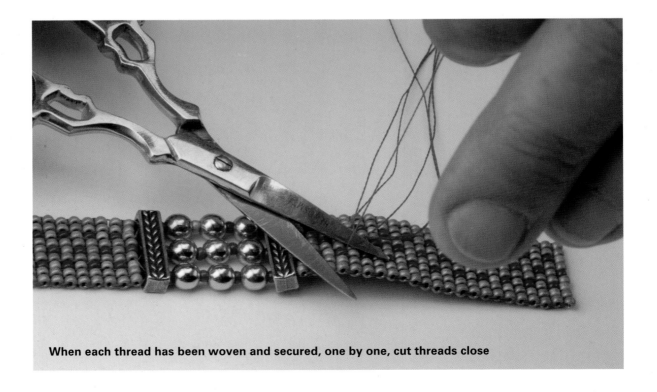

When each thread has been woven and secured, one by one, cut threads close

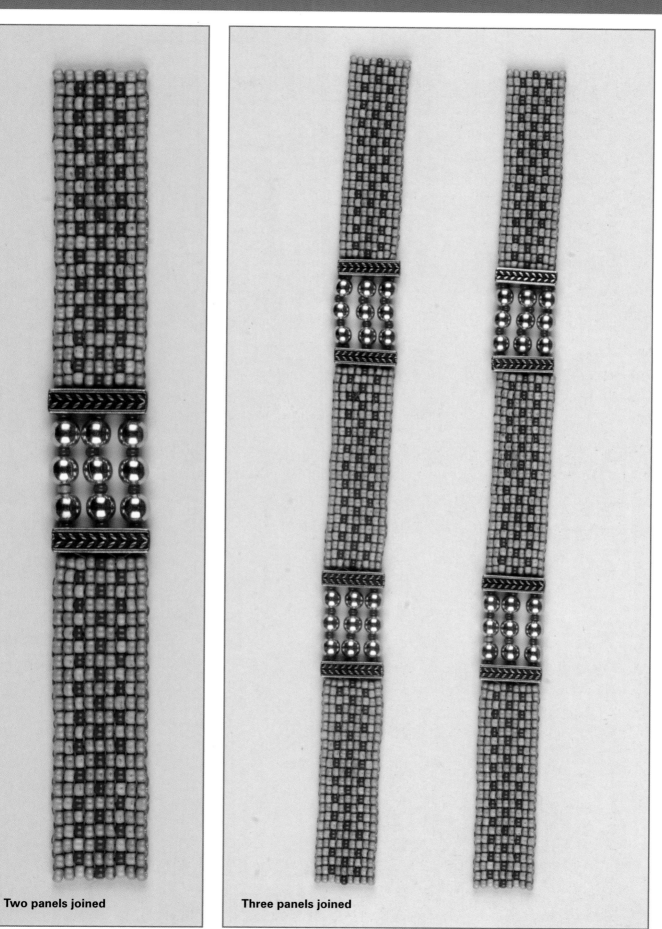

Two panels joined

Three panels joined

Choosing & Adding the Focal Bead

When selecting a focal bead it is best to keep three things in mind; color, shape and size. It was easy to dismiss the bright orange bead because the color was not close enough and the size too small, but harder to choose between the remaining two beads. I finally selected the bicone bead rather than the cylindrical one because not only did the bicone shape lend contrast to the broad, flat band of the necklace, the dots on the bicone also complimented the 4 mm round copper beads.

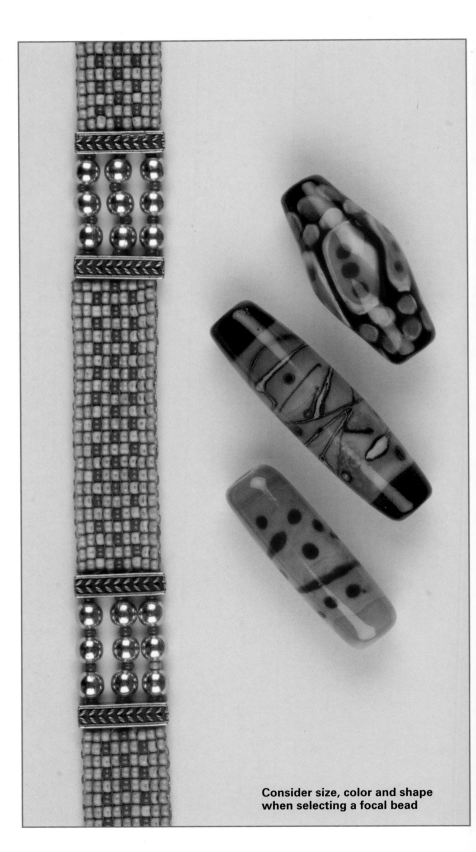

Consider size, color and shape when selecting a focal bead

Cut 3 lengths of thread each approximately 30" long. Following instructions from photos 4-04 through 4-09 add a copper spacer bar and accent beads. Do not use a second spacer bar. Secure the threads with an overhand knot. It is easy to put the knot close to the accent beads by moving it with a needle. The overhand knot will secure the accent beads.

Add the copper spacer bar and accent beads

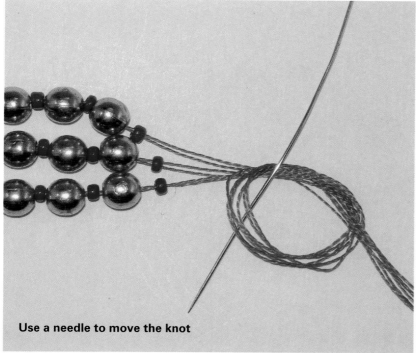

Use a needle to move the knot

Secure the knot close to the accent beads

Add one of the spacer beads, then separate the threads back into 3 sets of 2 threads each. String 3 DO seed beads onto each set of threads. Make the last seed bead a stop bead by passing the needle back through the last seed bead. Snug all the beads close. Add the focal bead.

Separate the threads back into 3 sets of 2 threads each. String 3 DO seed beads onto each set of threads. This time make the first seed bead a stop bead. Add the second set of accent beads and a spacer bar.

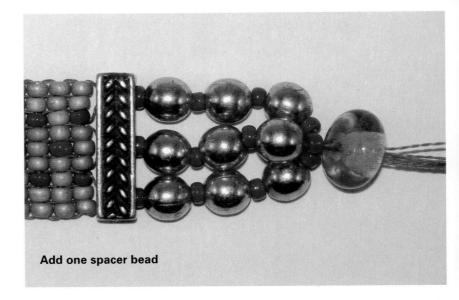

Add one spacer bead

Add three sets of seed beads

The complete centerpiece

Weave the threads into the next panel, each set of threads passing through 3 beads in opposite directions. Weave threads through the end row of the remaining panels, as if you were connecting panels.

Bring the threads together on the second row and tie each set of threads in a square knot.

Weave each of the 6 threads into the panel, being sure to take a back-stitch or two along the way to secure the threads. When each thread has been woven and secured, one by one cut the threads close.

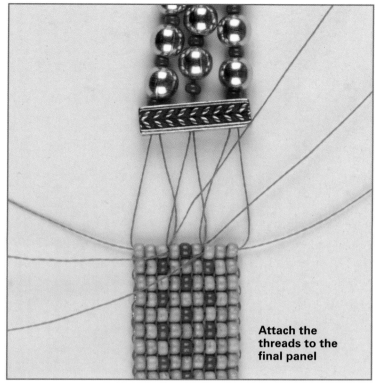

Attach the threads to the final panel

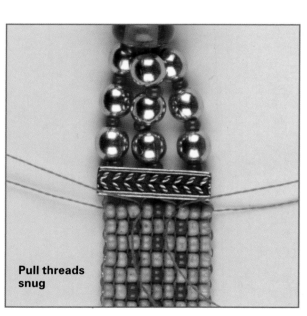

Pull threads snug

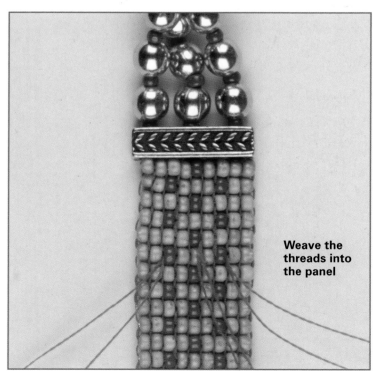

Weave the threads into the panel

Attaching The Clasp

Cut 3 lengths of thread each approximately 20" long. Following instructions from photos on pages 53 and 54 to add threads.

String on one copper 3-hole spacer bar. String on one DO seed bead, one 4 mm copper bead and one DO seed bead.

Pass the thread through both openings of a copper wire guard and pass the wire guard through one loop of the end bar. Do the same with the remaining 2 sets of threads.

Now bring the threads back through the seed beads and copper beads, back through the spacer bar and then back through the end row of beads.

Weave each of the 6 threads into the panel, being sure to take a backstitch or two along the way. When each thread has been woven and secured, one by one cut threads close.

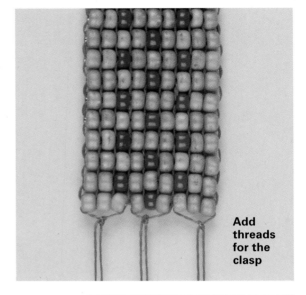

Add threads for the clasp

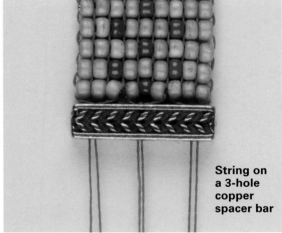

String on a 3-hole copper spacer bar

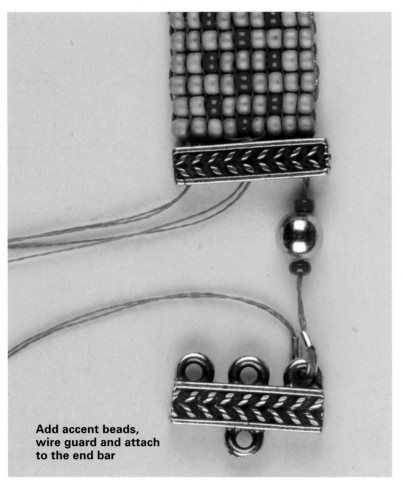

Add accent beads, wire guard and attach to the end bar

The wire guard attaches to the end bar

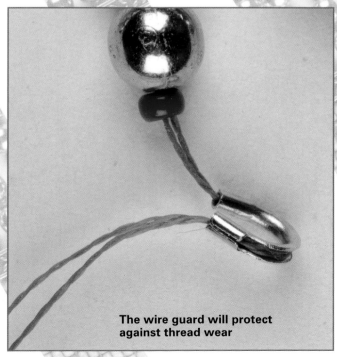

The wire guard will protect against thread wear

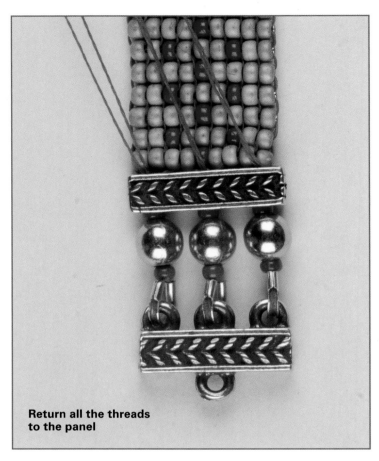

**Return all the threads
to the panel**

Weave threads into the panel to secure

To finish the necklace attach the toggle clasp to the end bar by using a jump ring. Open the jump ring by gently turning with two sets of pliers. Attach the jump ring to the loops on both the end bar and the clasp. Close the jump ring. Follow the same instructions for both sides.

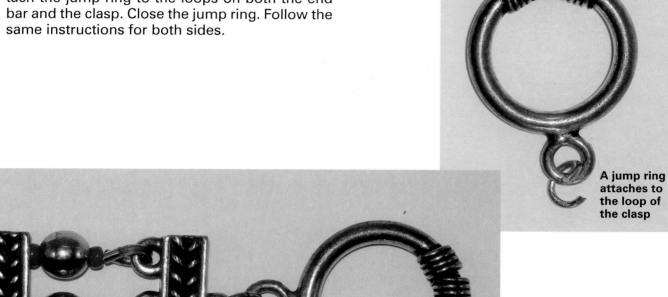

A jump ring attaches to the loop of the clasp

The jump ring secures the clasp to the end bar

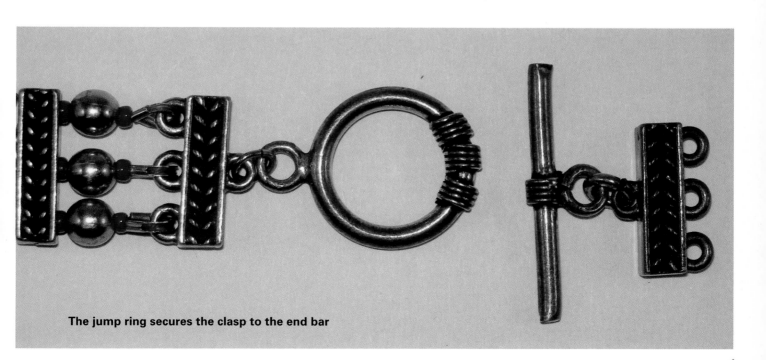

The jump ring secures the clasp to the end bar

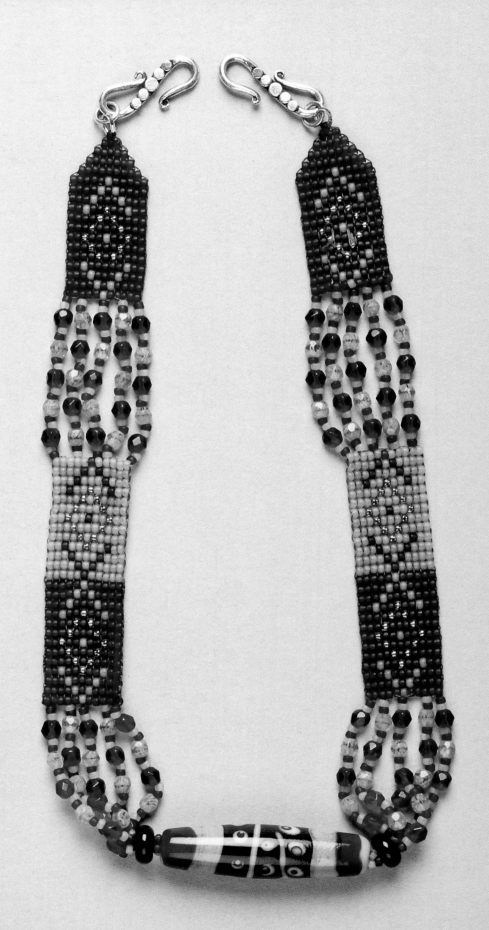

Blueberry Parfait Necklace

The colors in this pattern are just luscious and remind me of homemade blueberry ice cream. Accentuated by small cut glass beads, sterling silver and a stunning focal, this design is sheer elegance. For those who like a longer necklace, the option of an extension is offered.

Estimated Time to complete: Approximately 10 hours.

The techniques used in this necklace will teach how to weave panels together, add accent and focal beads, and how to attach a clasp.

Colors will be indicated as follows:
DB for dark blue
LB for light blue
GR for iridescent green

Instructions for the necklace extender are given separately.

Supplies for Necklace

1 pack Toho™ 11 round #8F bead or similar (**DB**)

1 pack Toho™ 11 round #146F bead or similar (**LB**)

1 pack Toho™ 11 round #164 bead or similar (**GR**)

1 focal bead

2 spacer beads, sized to fit the ends of the focal bead

52 dark blue, 3 - 4 mm accent beads

48 light blue, 3 - 4 mm accent beads

2 silver wire guards

2 silver jump rings

2 sterling silver "S" hooks with soldered rings

Beading needles size 12

40 yds. Silamide, royal blue #7669 waxed nylon beadstring, size A

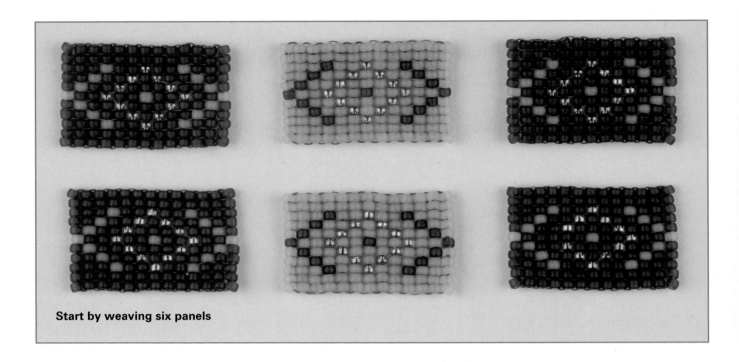

Start by weaving six panels

The Pattern

Start with two arms length of thread. Add a stop bead and anchor your thread. Begin by weaving six panels. Four panels will be predominantly dark blue and two panels will be predominantly light blue. Each panel will be 11 beads across and 13 rows down, measuring 1 inch long by 5/8 inch wide. Size adjustments may be made by adding an extension.

Blueberry Parfait Dark Blue Panel

1st row: 5 DB, 1 LB, 5 DB
2nd row: 4 DB, 1 LB, 1 DB, 1 LB, 4 DB
3rd row: 3 DB, 1 LB, 3 DB, 1 LB, 3 DB
4th row: 2 DB, 1 LB, 2 DB, 1 GR, 2 DB, 1 LB, 2 DB
5th row: 4 DB, 1 GR, 1 DB, 1 GR, 5 DB
6th row: 3 DB, 1 GR, 3 DB, 1 GR, 3 DB
7th row: 2 DB, 1 GR, 2 DB, 1 LB, 2 DB, 1 GR, 2 DB
8th row: 3 DB, 1 GR, 3 DB, 1 GR, 3 DB
9th row: 4 DB, 1 GR, 1 DB, 1 GR, 4 DB
10th row: 2 DB, 1 LB, 2 DB, 1 GR, 2 DB, 1 LB, 2 DB
11th row: 3 DB, 1 LB, 3 DB, 1 LB, 3 DB
12th row: 4 DB, 1 LB, 1 DB, 1 LB, 4 DB
13th row: 5 DB, 1 LB, 5 DB

Weave both tails of thread back into the panel being sure to take a backstitch or two along the way to secure the threads.

Blueberry Parfait Light Blue Panel

Start with two arms length of thread. Add on a stop bead and anchor your thread. Leave a 15 inch tail (not shown). This will be used to weave one dark blue and one light blue panel together.

1st row: 5 LB, 1 DB, 5 LB
2nd row: 4 LB, 1 DB, 1 LB, 1DB, 4 LB
3rd row: 3 LB, 1 DB, 3 LB, 1 DB, 3 LB
4th row: 2 LB, 1 DB, 2 LB, 1 GR, 2 LB, 1 DB, 2 LB
5th row: 4 LB, 1 GR, 1 LB, 1 GR, 4 LB
6th row: 3 LB, 1 GR, 3 LB, 1 GR, 3 LB
7th row: 2 LB, 1 GR, 2 LB, 1 DB, 2 LB, 1 GR, 2 LB
8th row: 3 LB, 1 GR, 3 LB, 1 GR, 3 LB
9th row: 4 LB, 1 GR, 1 LB, 1 GR, 4 LB
10th row: 2 LB, 1 DB, 2 LB, 1 GR, 2 LB, 1 DB, 2 LB
11th row: 3 LB, 1 DB, 3 LB, 1 DB, 3 LB
12th row: 4 LB, 1 DB, 1 LB, 1 DB, 4 LB
13th row: 5 LB, 1 DB, 5 LB

Weave one tail of thread back into the panel being sure to take a backstitch or two along the way to secure the threads.

Weave Triangle Ends On Two Blue Panels

Using a new length of thread, add five rows of dark blue beads to one end of the panel. Decrease by one bead at the start and one bead at the end of each row. The five rows will have 9, 7, 5, 3 and then 1 bead. Using approximately 30" of thread should give you enough to leave a 12" tail for adding the clasp.

14th row - 9 DB
15th row - 7 DB
16th row - 5 DB
17th row - 3 DB
18th row - 1 DB

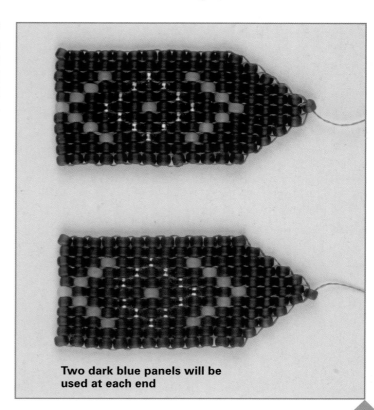

Two dark blue panels will be used at each end

Adding Threads For Accent Beads

The first set of accent beads will be added to the 2 dark blue panels with the triangle ends. Cut 5 lengths of thread each approximately 18" long for each panel. Thread a needle and pass thread #1 through 2 end beads, pulling through until the thread is an even length on both sides of the seed beads. Tie thread into a square knot. Do the same with the remaining 4 threads. Thread #2 will pass through next 2 beads, thread #3 through the middle 3 beads, thread #4 through the next 2 beads and thread #5 through the last 2 beads. Tie each thread with a square knot.

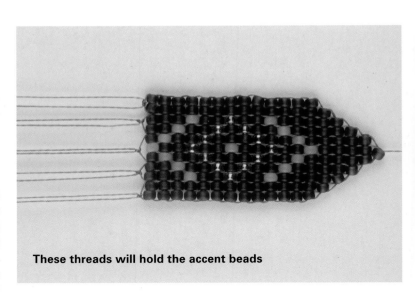

These threads will hold the accent beads

Adding The Accent Beads

Follow this pattern for threads 1, 3 and 5:
DB bead, LB bead, DB 4 mm accent bead, LB bead, DB bead, LB 4 mm accent bead.

Repeat until all beads are strung. Make the last seed bead of each strand a stop bead. This way the accent beads will not slip off the threads as you continue to work.

Follow this pattern for threads 2 and 4:
LB bead, DB bead, LB 4 mm accent bead, DB bead, LB bead, DB 4 mm accent bead.

Repeat until all beads are strung. Make the last seed bead of each strand a stop bead.

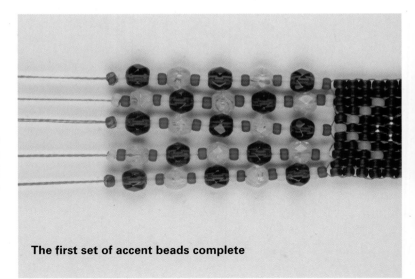

The first set of accent beads complete

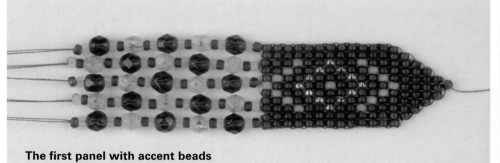

The first panel with accent beads

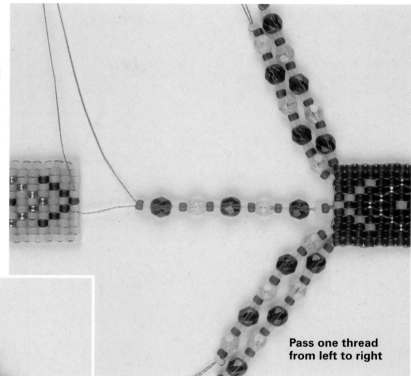

To attach the accent beads from the dark blue panel to the light blue panel, start with the middle threads on the dark blue panel. Undo the stop bead and separate the threads. Pass the threads through the three middle beads of the light blue panel, each thread going in the opposite direction.

Pass one thread from left to right

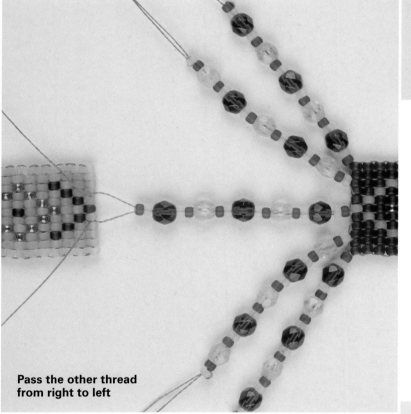

Pass the other thread from right to left

Do the same with the remaining 4 sets of threads, passing each thread through 2, not 3, beads. Bring each set of thread together on the second row and tie in a square knot.

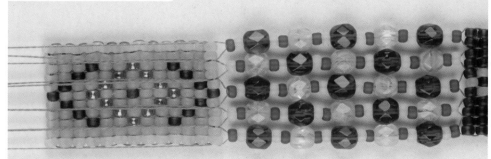

Bring all threads through the panel in sets

Reversing direction weave the 5 pairs of threads back through the bottom row of the light blue panel and back through the accent beads and into the dark blue panel. Tie each set of threads in a square knot.

Separate the threads and one thread at a time, weave each thread approximately six rows into the dark blue panel. Be sure to backstitch at least once for each thread. Once threads have been secured, trim close.

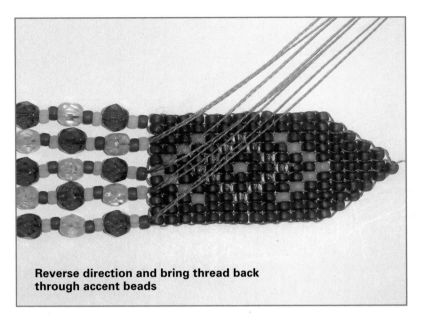

Reverse direction and bring thread back through accent beads

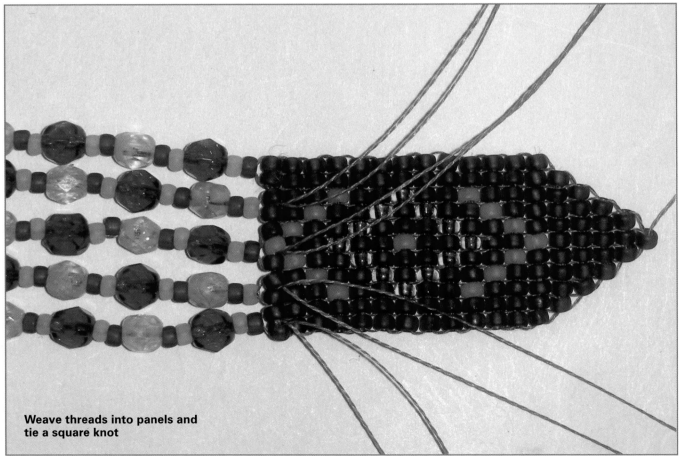

Weave threads into panels and tie a square knot

Making Some Decisions

My original intention was to construct the necklace by alternating the panels and accent beads. However, once the organization of the pieces started coming together, it became clear that joining the dark blue and light blue panels would give the design more interest.

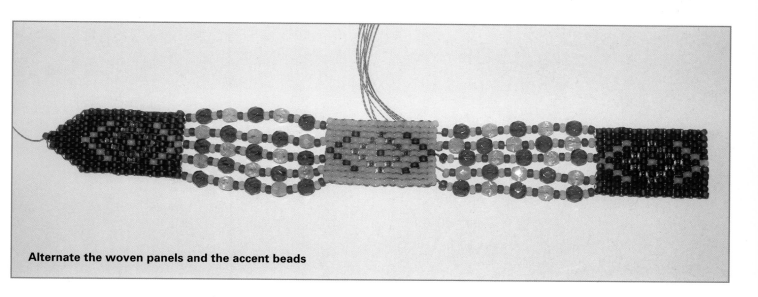

Alternate the woven panels and the accent beads

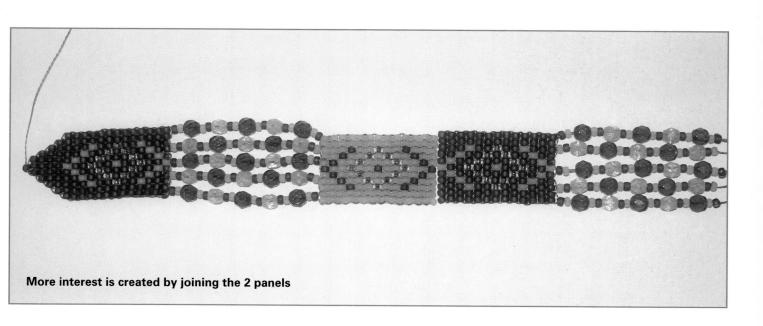

More interest is created by joining the 2 panels

Joining The Dark Blue and Light Blue Panels

Using the 12-inch tail of the light blue panel, pass the thread through the first bead of the dark blue panel. Return the thread through the end bead of the light blue panel.

Pass thread back through the first and second bead of the dark blue panel.

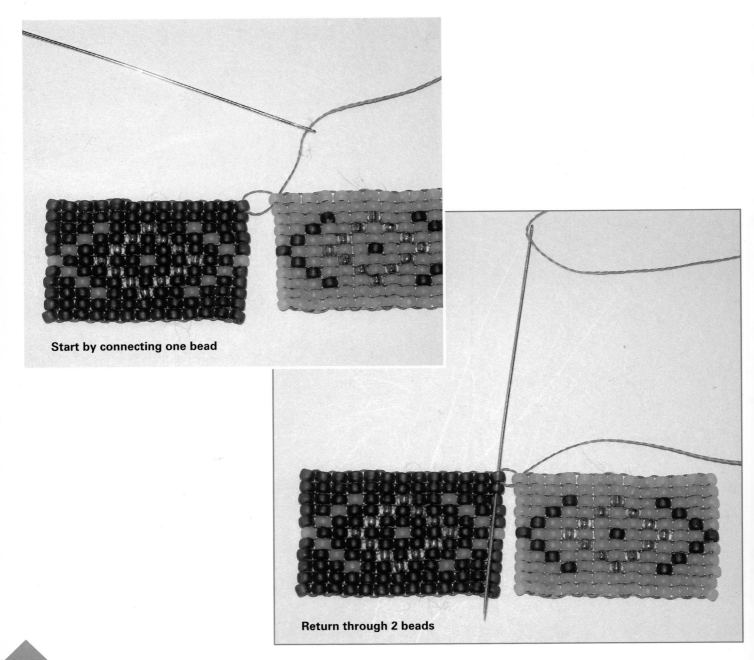

Start by connecting one bead

Return through 2 beads

Return thread through the last 2 beads of the light blue panel, and back through the first 3 beads of the dark blue panel. Continue stitching by passing thread back though two beads on the light blue panel and return through three beads on the dark blue panel, until you reach the end.

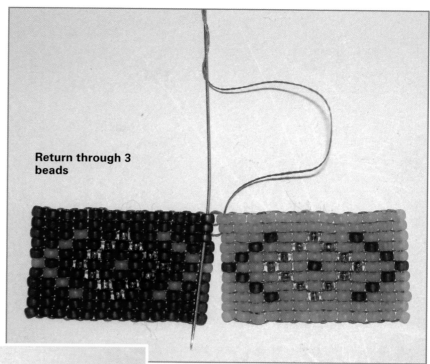

Return through 3 beads

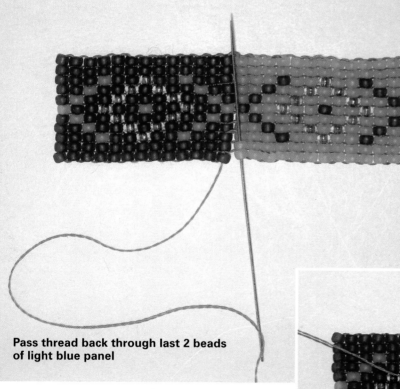

Pass thread back through last 2 beads of light blue panel

Pass the thread back through last two beads of LB panel. Reinforce with a couple of stitches, then back weave thread, being sure to take a back stitch or two and trim.

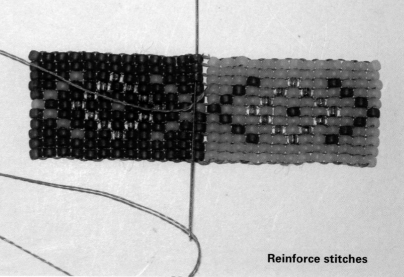

Reinforce stitches

Adding Threads For The
Second Set of Accent Beads

Complete 2 panels, each consisting of a dark blue end panel, a set of accent beads, a light blue panel, and another dark blue panel. You will be adding threads for accent beads to only one dark blue panel. Use longer threads this time, approximately 48 inches long. These threads will accommodate not only this set of accent beads, but the focal beads and the next set of accent beads as well. It is important to have enough thread to complete this step, so if in doubt, use more, not less. You can always trim the excess thread.

Follow directions for "Adding Threads for Accent Beads," to add the 5 sets of threads, as shown on page 78.

Add a second set of accent beads

String the accent beads following directions from "Adding the Accent Beads." Make the last bead a stop bead at the end of each row. This will secure the work and keep the accent beads in place. When all beads are strung, tie an overhand knot. Snug the knot close to the accent beads.

Add one spacer bead. Now separate the threads back into 5 sets of 2 threads each and add 2 more seed beads per thread, following the same sequence. Make the end seed bead be a stop bead. Add the focal bead.

Add a spacer bead

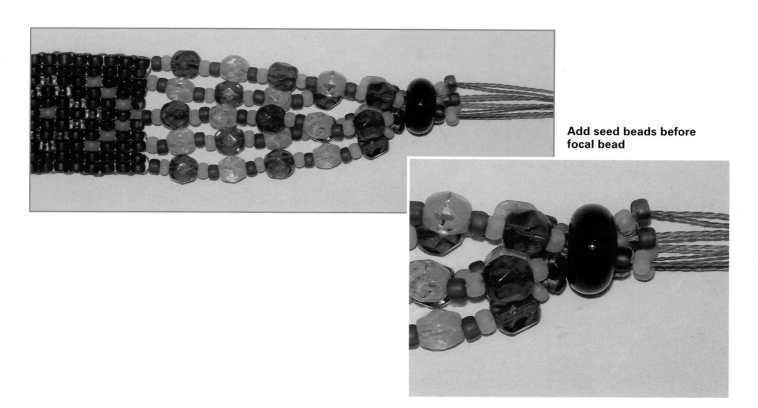

Add seed beads before focal bead

Add the focal bead

Separate the threads back into 5 sets of 2 threads each. Add another 2 seed beads following the same sequence. This time make the first bead on each set a stop bead. Using all threads, tie an overhand knot and snug the knot close to the seed beads. Add the second spacer bead.

Add seed beads after focal bead

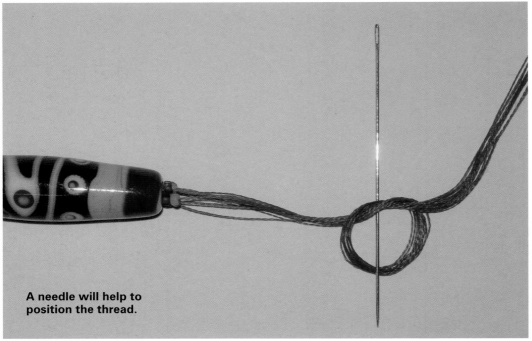

A needle will help to position the thread.

Add a spacer bead

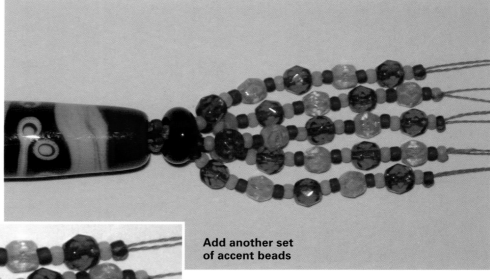

Separate the threads back into 5 sets of 2 threads each. String the remaining accent beads in the reverse direction. Start each set of beads with a stop bead. This will keep your work secure. End each set of beads with a stop bead which will be removed one by one when you attach the threads to the next panel.

Add another set of accent beads

Thread by thread, undo the stop beads and bring each set of threads through the 2 corresponding beads of the dark blue panel. The threads should run through the beads in opposite directions. The middle set of threads will run through the 3 middle beads.

Bring the threads together on the second row and tie each set of threads in a square knot to secure. One thread at a time, weave the 5 pairs of threads through the dark blue panel for at least 5 rows. Be sure to backstitch one or two times along the way. Trim all threads close.

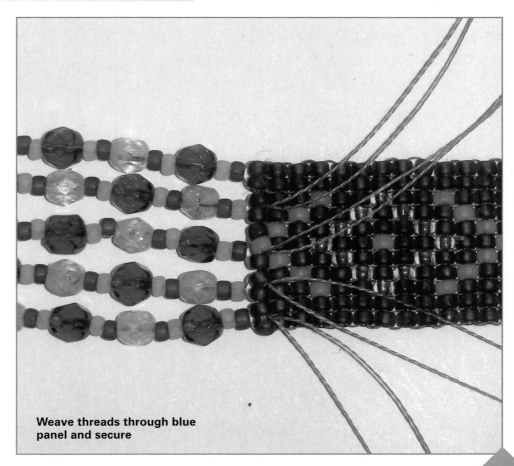

Weave threads through blue panel and secure

Adding The "S" Hook

Thread a needle onto the tail of a triangle. Pass the thread through each end opening of a silver wire guard. Pass the needle and thread through the soldered ring of a sterling silver "S" hook. Return the thread back through the end bead of the triangle. Pull the thread snug to tighten. Take several stitches through the wire guard and the last bead of the triangle before weaving the thread back into the panel.

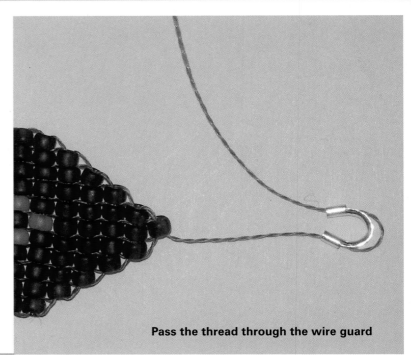

Pass the thread through the wire guard

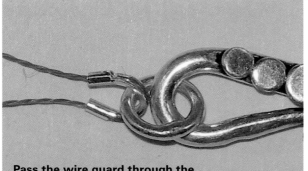

Pass the wire guard through the soldered ring of an "S" hook

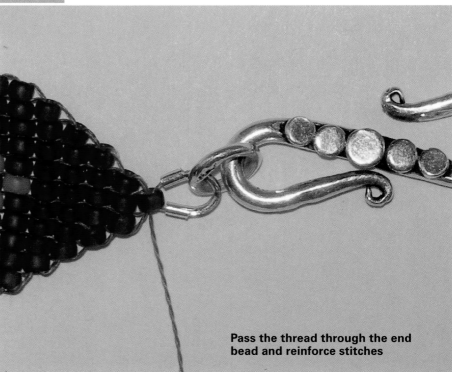

Pass the thread through the end bead and reinforce stitches

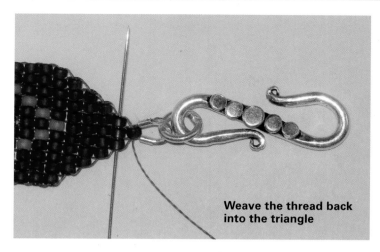

Weave the thread back into the triangle

Continue weaving back

Row by row, weave the thread back through the triangle passing the thread through all the beads of the row. This extra thread will give strength to the area and help keep the clasp secure.

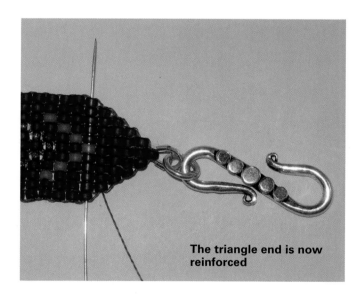

The triangle end is now reinforced

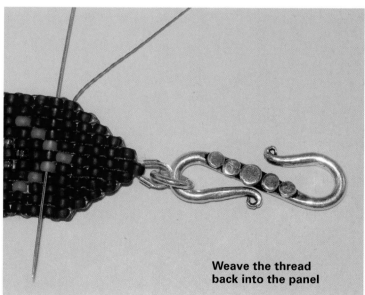

Weave the thread back into the panel

When you have passed the triangle area, bring the thread out in the middle of the work. Continue to weave the thread back into the panel. Take two backstitches along the way to secure the thread. When the thread is secured, trim close.

Add the second "S" hook in the same manner. Your finished necklace is now ready to wear.

Note: Instructions for the necklace extension follow.

Necklace Extension

Supplies for Extension

1 pack Toho™ 11 round #8F seed bead or similar (**DB**)

1 pack Toho™ 11 round #146F seed bead or similar (**LB**)

48 dark blue, 3 - 4 mm accent beads

47 light blue, 3 - 4 mm accent beads

2 silver crimp beads, size #2

2 sterling silver "S" hooks with soldered rings

Beading needles #12

5 yds. Silamide, royal blue #7669 waxed nylon beadstring, size A

The Pattern

Cut five lengths of thread, 36" long each.

String threads 1, 2 and 3 in the following order:

1 DB, 1 LB, 1 dark blue accent bead, 1 LB, 1 DB, 1 light blue accent bead

Repeat until you have strung 10 dark blue accent beads and 9 light blue accent beads on each thread. End with 1 LB bead and then 1 DB bead.

String threads 4 and 5 in the following order:

1 LB, 1 DB, 1 light blue accent bead, 1 DB, 1 LB, 1 dark blue accent bead

Repeat until you have strung 10 light blue accent beads and 9 dark blue accent beads on each thread. End with 1 DB bead and then 1 DB bead.

Gather all thread together and tie an overhand knot in each end.

To finish the ends, slide a #2 silver crimp bead over all 5 sets of thread. Pass the threads through the soldered ring of the "S" hook. Return the threads through the crimp bead. Tie an overhand knot and pull knot as close to the beads as possible. Position the crimp bead over the knot.

Add the crimp bead

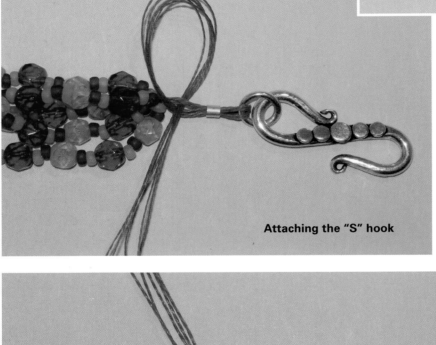

Attaching the "S" hook

Tie an overhand knot

Crimp the crimp bead using crimping pliers. Using the second set of notches crimp to a fold. Using the first set of notches, tighten the crimp bead.

The crimp bead

The secure crimp bead

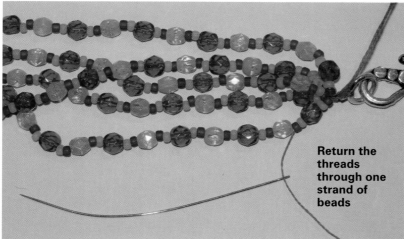

Return the threads through one strand of beads

One by one, return all threads back through one row of beads. Using only one row will keep the threads secure. Tie an overhand knot along the way, then continue returning the thread. When all threads have been passed through a row of beads, trim close.

The extension is now complete. Attach to the necklace with the "S" hooks.

When all threads are secure, trim close

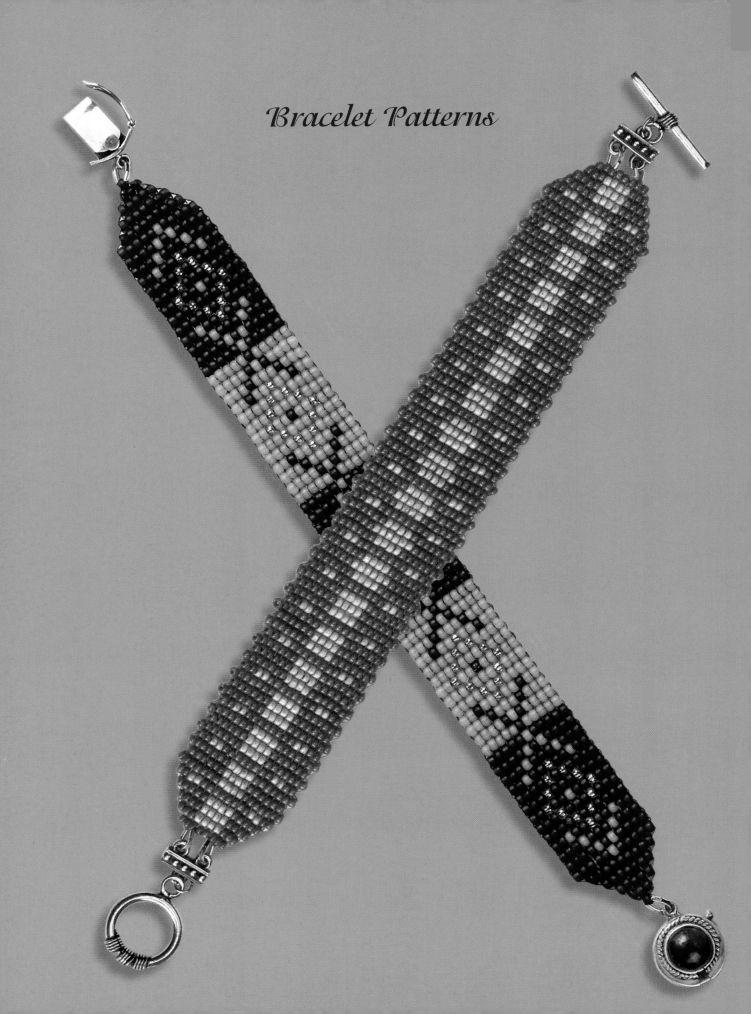

Bracelet Patterns

Blueberry Bracelet

The Blueberry bracelet is woven following the same pattern as the Blueberry Parfait necklace, only this time as a continuous panel. Weave the panel first and then add the triangle ends. The finished panel will measure 11/16" wide by 6" long. The clasp used adds another inch making the bracelet 7" long. The pattern can not be easily shortened but may be lengthened by adding additional rows of dark blue seed beads before adding the triangle.

Estimated time to complete: 4 hours

Supplies

1 pack Toho™ 11 round #8F bead or similar (**DB**)

1 pack Toho™ 11 round #146F bead or similar (**LB**)

1 pack Toho™ 11 round #164 bead or similar (**GR**)

2 silver wire guards

2 silver jump rings

1 sterling silver clasp

Beading needles #12

20 yds. Silamide, royal blue #7669 waxed nylon beadstring, size A

The Pattern

Begin with a stop bead and anchor your thread. String on 11 beads.

Row 1: 5 DB, 1 LB, 5 DB
Row 2: 4 DB, 1 LB, 1 DB, 1 LB, 4 DB
Row 3: 3 DB, 1 LB, 3 DB, 1 LB, 3 DB
Row 4: 2 DB, 1 LB, 2 DB, 1 GR, 2 DB, 1 LB, 2 DB
Row 5: 4 DB, 1 GR, 1 DB, 1 GR, 4 DB
Row 6: 3 DB, 1 GR, 3 DB, 1 GR, 3 DB
Row 7: 2 DB, 1 GR, 2 DB, 1 LB, 2 DB, 1 GR, 2 DB
Row 8: 3 DB, 1 GR, 3 DB, 1 GR, 3 DB
Row 9: 4 DB, 1 GR, 1 DB, 1 GR, 4 DB
Row 10: 2 DB, 1 LB, 2 DB, 1 GR, 2 DB, 1 LB, 2 DB
Row 11: 3 DB, 1 LB, 3 DB, 1 LB, 3 DB
Row 12: 4 DB, 1 LB, 1 DB, 1 LB, 4 DB
Row 13: 5 DB, 1 LB, 5 DB
Row 14: 5 LB, 1 DB, 5 LB
Row 15: 4 LB, 1 DB, 1 LB, 1 DB, 4 LB
Row 16: 3 LB, 1 DB, 3 LB, 1 DB, 3 LB
Row 17: 2 LB, 1 DB, 2 LB, 1 GR, 2 LB, 1 DB, 2 LB
Row 18: 4 LB, 1 GR, 1 LB, 1 GR, 4 LB
Row 19: 3 LB, 1 GR, 3 LB, 1 GR, 3 LB
Row 20: 2 LB, 1 GR, 2 LB, 1 DB, 2 LB, 1 GR, 2 LB
Row 21: 3 LB, 1 GR, 3 LB, 1 GR, 3 LB
Row 22: 4 LB, 1 GR, 1 LB, 1 GR, 4 LB
Row 23: 2 LB, 1 DB, 2 LB, 1 GR, 2 LB, 1 DB, 2 LB
Row 24: 3 LB, 1 DB, 3 LB, 1 DB, 3 LB
Row 25: 4 LB, 1 DB, 1 LB, 1 DB, 4 LB
Row 26: 5 LB, 1 DB, 5 LB
Repeat rows 1 through 26
Repeat rows 1 through 13

After the last row, decrease evenly to form a triangle by adding four rows of dark blue beads. Decrease by one bead at the start and one bead at the end of each row. Plan to have enough thread to leave a 12" tail for adding the clasp.

Row 66: 9 DB
Row 67: 7 DB
Row 68: 5 DB
Row 69: 3 DB

Add a triangle to the other side of the panel following the instructions above.

Decrease to form triangle ends.

The bracelet panel

Adding The Clasp

String a wire guard onto the 12 inch tail.

Slide the loop end of the clasp over the wire guard.

Return the thread through the last 3 beads.

Reinforce by passing the thread through the thread guard several times.

Then weave the thread back and forth through 4 rows through the triangle, passing the needle through all the beads on each row.

After passing the 5th row, bring the needle out in the middle of the work.

Stitch back another 6 rows, taking one or two backstitches along the way.

When thread is secured, trim close.
Repeat for the 2nd half of the clasp.

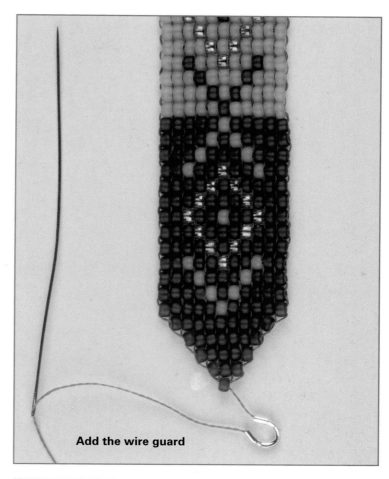

Add the wire guard

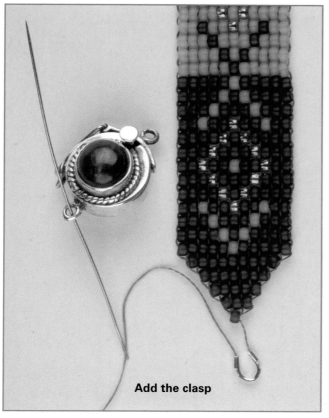

Add the clasp

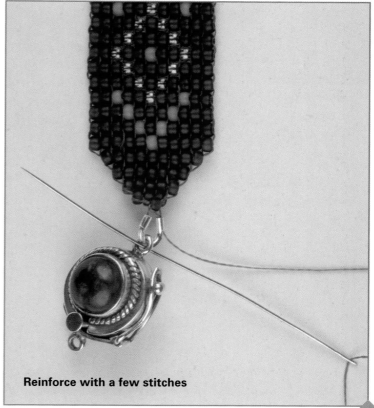

Reinforce with a few stitches

Start to weave thread back

When threads are secure, trim close.

"Stepping Stones" Bracelet

The Stepping Stones bracelet is an easy way to practice increasing and decreasing stitches. This pattern changes in the middle, adding a subtle focal point to the center of the design. The finished panel will measure 3-1/8 inches wide by 6-1/2 inches long. The end bars and clasp add another 1-1/2 inches, resulting in a bracelet 8 inches long. The pattern can easily be lengthened or shortened by adjusting the repeat of the pattern.

Estimated time to complete: 4 hours

Supplies

1 pack Toho™ 11 round #46L bead or similar (**DO**)

1 pack Toho™ 11 round #562F bead or similar (**LO**)

1 pack Toho™ 11 round #557F bead or similar (**G**)

4 - copper wire guards

2 - 2 hole copper end bars

2 - copper jump rings

1 - copper toggle clasp

Beading needles #12

1 pack Silamide, gold #7290 waxed nylon beadstring, size A

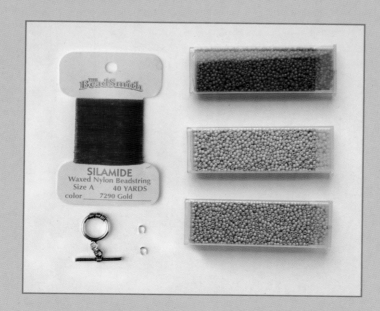

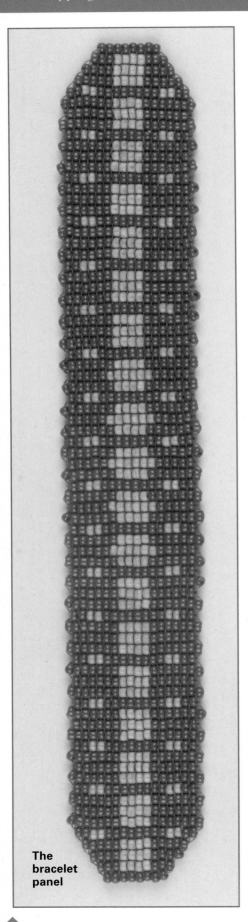

The bracelet panel

The Pattern

Row 1: 8 DO
Row 2: 3 DO, 4 G, 3 DO
Row 3: 4 DO, 4 G, 4 DO
Row 4: 5 DO, 4 G, 5 DO
Row 5: 2 DO, 2 LO, 8 DO, 2 LO, 2 DO
Row 6: 7 DO, 4 G, 7 DO
Row 7: 6 DO, 4 G, 6 DO
Row 8: 7 DO, 4 G, 7 DO
Row 9: 2 DO, 2 LO, 8 DO, 2 LO, 2 DO
Rows 10 - 29: Repeat rows 6, 7, 8 and 9
Row 30: 7 DO, 4 G, 7 DO
Row 31: 5 DO, 1 LO, 1 G, 2 DO, 1 G, 1 LO, 5 DO
Row 32: 7 DO, 4 G, 7 DO
Row 33: 2 DO, 2 LO, 8 DO, 2 LO, 2 DO
Rows 34 - 39: Repeat rows 30, 31, 32 and 33
Rows 50 - 73: Repeat rows 6, 7, 8 and 9
Row 74: 5 DO, 4 G, 5 DO
Row 75: 4 DO, 4 G, 4 DO
Row 76: 3 DO, 4 G, 3 DO
Row 77: 8 DO

Adding The Clasp

Start with 18 inches of thread. Pass threaded needle through two beads on the end row, skipping the last bead. Pass the needle through the wire guard. Pass the wire guard onto a loop on the end bar. Place a needle on the other end of the thread and bring the thread through the same two beads in the opposite direction. Bring threads together on the next row and tie using a square knot.

Weave both threads back through the panel, securing with several backstitches along the way. When thread is secured, trim close.

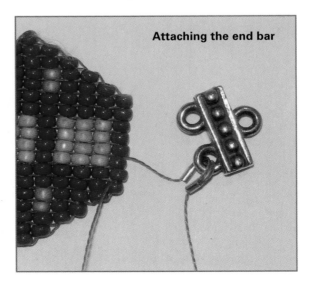

Attaching the end bar

Both wire guards attached

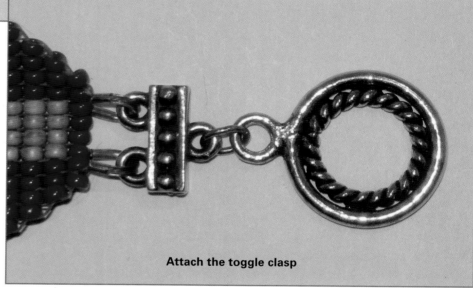

Attach the toggle clasp

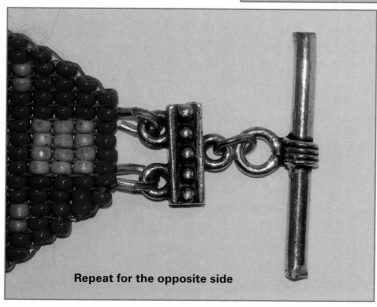

Repeat for the opposite side

Gallery
Ideas for Inspiration

Once you have mastered the square stitch, you might be anxious to learn some new stitches. The gallery photos show what is possible, using simple techniques combined with imagination.

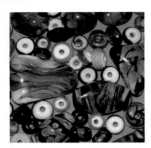

Judy Donovan, Philadelphia, Pennsylvania.
Bead embroidered collar featuring 5 dichroic
cabochons designed and made by the artist.

Marilyn Elliott, Portland, Oregon.
Peyote stitch collar using Toho™
Treasures and free-form pearl accents.

Judy Donovan, Philadelphia, Pennsylvania. Strung pearls and accent beads supporting an embroidered and embellished taxidermy eye, all of which provides protection for the wearer.

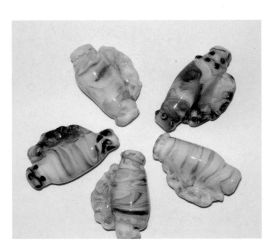

Victoria Gray Harding and *Harry Harding*, Pennsauken, New Jersey. Brick stitch leaves and embellished silk cord using Toho™ Triangle beads.

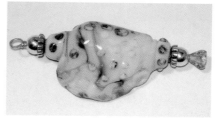

Kim Tamarin, Boring, Oregon. Free-form peyote stitch using Toho™ Treasures with a focal stone.

Judy Donovan, Philadelphia, Pennsylvania. Embroidered ssilk necklace cord with a suspended clay face by Barbara Hanselman, Cherry Hill, NJ. Various seed and accent bead embellishments are featured.

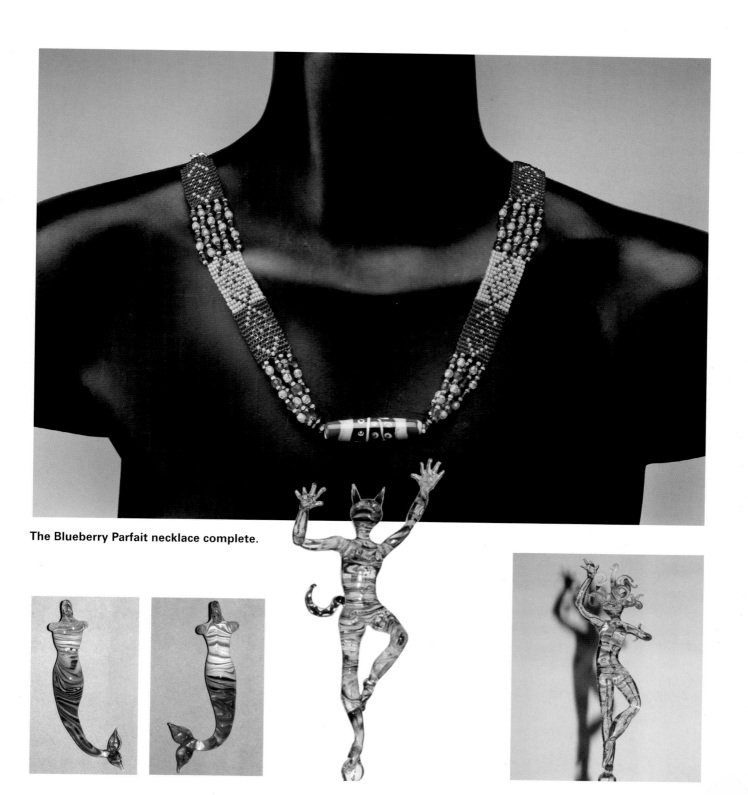

The Blueberry Parfait necklace complete.

The Purple Mountains necklace complete.

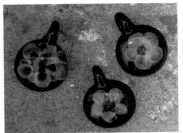

The Autumn Harvest necklace complete.

Index